Indian FOOD
& FOLKLORE

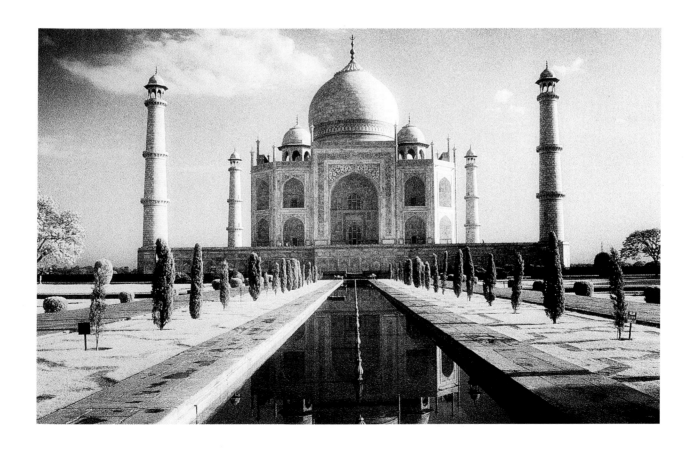

Indian FOOD
& FOLKLORE

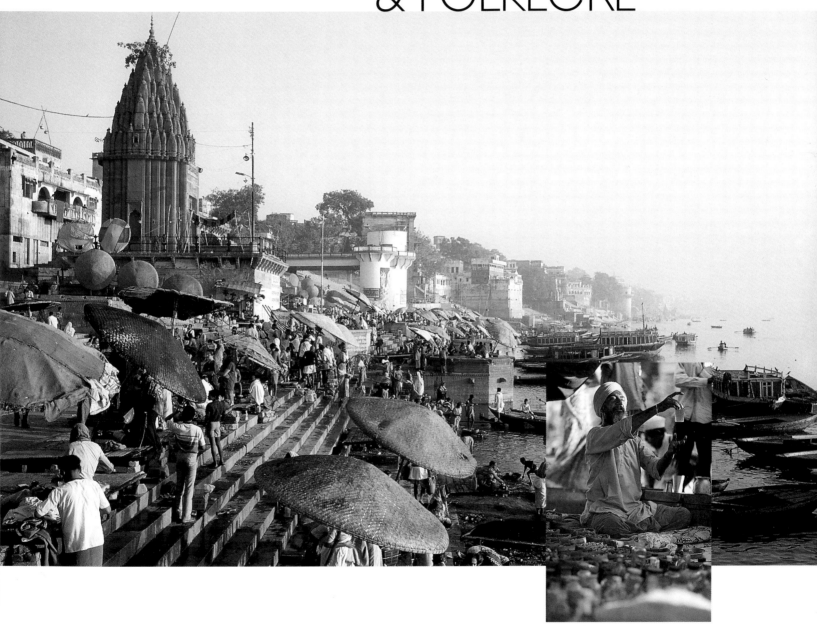

hamlyn

Editor Cara Frost
Copy Editor Jo Lethaby
Art Director Keith Martin
Designer Claire Harvey
Production Controller Katherine Hockley

Contributors
Photographer Ian Wallace
Home Economist Eliza Baird
Stylist Clare Hunt
Picture Researcher Liz Fowler
Indexer Pamela Le Gassick

Acknowledgements
AKG, London: Paul Almasy 6, 70
Corbis UK Ltd: Hulton-Getty Collection 8, 9, 18, 31, 51, 141 / Karan
Kapoor 38 / Earl Kowall 41, 108 / Craig Lovell 11, 23, 62, 123 / Hans
George Roth 119 / Bradley Smith 124 / Nevada Wier 35
Octopus Publishing Group Ltd: Ian Wallace 14, 15, 21, 25, 29, 33, 37,
43, 47, 53, 57, 61, 65, 69, 73, 75, 81, 85, 89, 93, 97, 99, 103, 107, 113,
117, 121, 129, 131, 134, 139
Robert Harding Picture Library: 3 insert, 59, 77, 87, 100, 125, 133 /
Jeremy Bright 82 / Alain Evrard 110 / T. Gervis 45 / Michael Short 83 /
Claude Wilson 49 / J.H.C. Wilson 17, 30, 115
Image Bank: Carlos Navajas 12 / Anne Rippy 78 / Harald Sand 54 /
Stephen Wilkes 5, 26
Tony Stone Images: Steward Cohen 66 / Will Curtis 1, 144 /
Nicholas DeVore 7, 104 / David Hanson 94 / Paul Harris 16 / Gavin
Hellier 126 / Chris Noble 136 / Martin Salter 10 /
David Sutherland 3 main picture, 91

Jacket credits
Will Curtis jacket wrap-around / T. Gervis front flap top /
David Hanson back flap top
Octopus Publishing Group Ltd: Ian Wallace front jacket insert

Indian Food & Folklore

First published in 2000 by Hamlyn
an imprint of Octopus Publishing Group Limited
2–4 Heron Quays, London E14 4JP

Copyright © 2000 Octopus Publishing Group Limited

British Library Cataloguing-in-Publication Data
A catalogue record for this book is available from the British Library

ISBN 0 600 59860 8

Printed in China by Toppan Printing Co., (H.K.) Ltd.

NOTES
Standard level spoon measurements are used in all recipes.
1 tablespoon = one 15 ml spoon
1 teaspoon = one 5 ml spoon

*Both imperial and metric measurements have been given
in all recipes. Use one set of measurements only and not a
mixture of both.*

Eggs should be medium unless otherwise stated.

*Ovens should be preheated to the specified temperature
– if using a fan assisted oven, follow the manufacturer's
instructions for adjusting the time and temperature.*

Contents

introduction

India is such a vast country that the style of cooking varies enormously from region to region. Geography – climate and soil – and local produce have played a big part in forming regional culinary traditions. Religious groups have modified the regional cuisines even further to suit their own beliefs and restrictions. History, too, has had a role and outsiders have all left their mark on Indian food and cooking – from the Moguls with their Persian style of cooking to the Portuguese, who ruled Goa on the west coast for four centuries and converted many people to Catholicism, and the British colonialists of the Raj who also left dishes in their wake.

RELIGION

Nearly 85 per cent of India's population are Hindu, while another 11 per cent are Muslims. Other faiths account for the rest of the population and include Jainism, Buddhism, Sikhism, Christianity and Zoroastrianism. Many of the various religions have had a role in shaping Indian cooking. Hindus, for example, have a religious fondness for bright red and yellow, which is reflected in their use of saffron and turmeric; while in the past 'impure' dishes could be purified by pouring ghee (clarified butter) over the top. Hindus offer food and drink to their gods and goddesses to show devotion, and some stone figures have become so coated with melted ghee and turmeric by pilgrims that they have lost their features. The gods are known to have their preferences – elephant-headed Ganesh, for example, favours sweets flavoured with cardamom.

Hindus regard the cow as sacred and therefore do not eat beef, while Muslims will not eat pork. Jains are strictly vegetarian and believe everything possesses life. Some Jains are so orthodox that they refrain from eating beetroot and tomatoes because the colour is similar to that of blood. They also exclude from their diet root vegetables such as garlic, onions, carrots, potatoes and ginger because the roots have a potential to grow.

SPICES

Bearing in mind the regional differences in Indian cooking, the common denominator

Certainly, Indian cooking is characterized by the use of a greater range of spices than any other cuisine. While the food is always spicy in flavour, it is not necessarily hot. The heat in Indian food in fact comes from hot chilli peppers, which were only introduced to Asia in the 16th century by the Portuguese who had discovered them in the New World.

Indian cooks may use the spices whole, they may fry or roast them, or perhaps grind them with water or vinegar to make a paste. Each technique draws out a completely different flavour from the same spice. In this way spices add variety to a diet of basic staple ingredients and the permutations become endless. In the ancient Indian Ayurvedic (Science of Life) system of medicine, spices are used not only for flavouring. They are prescribed in order to alleviate or prevent medical problems, enhance mood or trigger a physical reaction. Some are valued for their vitamin content and others, such as fenugreek, asafoetida and fresh ginger, for their use in combating flatulence in a diet based on pulses and starchy vegetables.

CURRY & CURRY POWDER

The word 'curry' is thought to be a corruption of the Tamil, or southern Indian word, karhi, which means sauce. Alternatively, it may have come from karhai or karahi,

a commonly used two-handled Indian cooking vessel similar to a wok. The curries first encountered by Europeans, from whom we have written accounts, seem to have been of a fairly liquid consistency, usually described as a broth or soup, poured over rice.

Throughout the days of the Raj, the term 'curry' evolved as a loose description of any Indian food cooked in a sauce. The early merchants and soldiers who visited India and enjoyed the richly spiced Indian dishes were keen to introduce the flavour when they returned home. Demand for a commercial curry powder developed over decades, and such spice mixtures have slowly become better in quality, blending different spices according to the seasonings used in different regions. However, curry powder as such is not a traditional authentic ingredient

in Indian cooking, and certainly does not exist in India. Most traditional households use individual spices, which are freshly ground and mixed as and when needed. The various blends used reflect the availability of the spices and the climate of the region to which they are accredited. Spice blends from the hotter regions contain more fiery chilli flavours, for example, while mixtures from cooler, northern climes usually concentrate on more fragrant flavours.

EARLY INDIAN CULTURE

It is known from archaeological evidence that a highly sophisticated, urbanized culture, the Indus civilization, dominated the north-west part of the subcontinent from about 2600 to 2000 BC. An Aryan or 'Indo-European' civilization from the Eurasian steppes – dominated by peoples with linguistic affinities to groups in Iran and Europe – moved into India from about 1700 BC onwards. They occupied the north-west first – in what is now the Punjab – and then north-central India, and subsequently spread southward and eastward at the expense of various indigenous groups. The Aryans' cultural and religious beliefs, based on their ancient Vedic scriptures, were mixed with those of the existing population and gradually laid the foundations of Indian society and the Hindu faith, with its caste system and belief in reincarnation.

The status of the cow

With the arrival of the Aryans, livestock – cattle in particular – assumed greater importance, and they appear to have introduced a heavy dependence on dairy produce.

The Aryans' diet included milk and curds – the latter being a popular food in a hot climate where its slight tartness was refreshing – and they cooked with ghee (clarified butter), which unlike fresh butter can be kept for months, even in a hot climate.

The Aryans brought their own cattle with them but these were gradually superseded by the native Indian breed, which was better adapted to the climate. The latter gave less milk, however, and as the indigenous people adopted dairy products with enthusiasm, demand probably outstripped supply. It therefore became necessary to protect the cow with the fullest sanctity of religious law. This belief in the sacredness of the cow and dairy products slowly diffused throughout the whole of the subcontinent.

In time, the law against cattle slaughter was relaxed and by about 700 BC it was generally accepted that cattle could be killed in the name of hospitality or in sacrifice to the gods and spirits. However, the increasing pressure on farmers for their valuable draft and milk animals by priests demanding cattle for ritual sacrifice provoked a strong social reaction and led to the emergence of two new religions – Buddhism and Jainism. Both sects opposed ritual sacrifice; they believed in the sanctity of all life and advocated vegetarianism. So influential was their anti-slaughter campaign that by the first century BC even the Brahmin priests of the orthodox Vedic faith had come round again and all three religions agreed that the cow was sacred.

EXTERNAL INFLUENCES ON COOKING

In the early centuries of the first millennium AD it appears that Indians ate two meals a day. The daily diet depended on the part of the country in which people lived. Wheat and barley could be grown in winter only in the south but at almost any time of the year in the cooler parts of the north. Rice was the standard crop on southern plains where there was irrigation. Gourds, peas, beans and lentils were found throughout the country and sugar cane, tamarind and mango were widely grown. Although rice, local spices, vegetables and fish were the base of south Indian cooking, the food was subject to many outside influences arriving by sea. To the repertoire of spices already used – pepper, cardamom and ginger – coriander and cumin were introduced to India's Malabar coast from the eastern Mediterranean via trade with the Arab world and Rome. On the other side of the subcontinent, the east-facing Coromandel coast had contact with the islands of Asia and with China, and imported from there nutmeg, mace and cloves.

While the Indian coasts received visitors by sea, in north-western India foreign contact came overland, through the passes of the Hindu Kush, in a succession of invasions and infiltrations of ideas, attitudes and techniques over thousands of years. Aryan, Persian, Greek and Central Asian influences were all absorbed into the heritage of the Indus Valley civilization to produce a mixed culture. Because the land was fertile and many of the influences nomadic, meat was more commonly eaten here than anywhere else in India.

The arrival of Islam

Islam, too, came from the north-west, brought to India by successive Arab, Turkish and Persian invaders from the early eighth century AD onwards. The first Muslims brought with them their everyday foods and cooking methods, but it was the establishment of a Muslim imperial power in India in the 16th century – that of the Moguls – that had many far-reaching effects on both Indian society and food. At the court of the Moguls a

new haute cuisine was introduced – a style of cooking derived from the Persians. Kebabs, pilaf or pilau dishes of rice with shredded meat, the technique of mixing fruits into meat dishes, the use of almonds and almond milk, rose petals, rosewater and the garnishing of all kinds of food with fragile strips of tissue beaten out of pure gold and silver (varq) were all absorbed into the Indian cuisine. Although Islam allowed Muslims to eat beef, their cuisine was based mainly on mutton and chicken, and non-vegetarian Hindus were therefore able to adopt it easily. The later Moguls made generous use of the chillies

first introduced by the Portuguese.

It was in the north, the heartland of Mogul rule, that Muslim food became most common. Even today, the cooking of the Punjab has almost as many links with the food of the Near East as with that of traditional India. One innovation that did spread from northern India throughout the whole subcontinent was the Muslim addiction to sweetmeats. Confections of all kinds, made from sugar alone or sugar with coconut, rice flour or with almonds, became immensely popular, as did sweet desserts such as jallebi.

EUROPEAN INFLUENCES

After the arrival in India of the Portuguese navigator, Vasco da Gama, in 1498 and the subsequent establishment of European maritime supremacy, India was exposed to more influences arriving by sea, lured by the trade in spices.

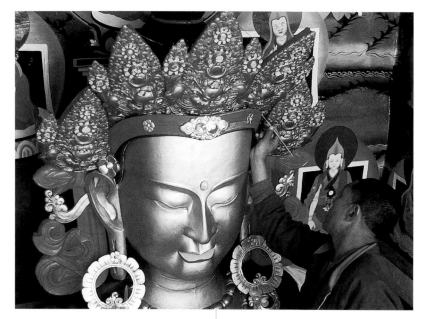

Thus with the arrival of the English, French, Portuguese, Dutch and Danish there began the development of Hindu-Muslim-European cuisine, now simply known as 'Indian'. The Portuguese brought from the New World chilli and capsicum peppers, tomatoes, cashew nuts, pineapple and papaya. The British introduced Northern European vegetables to India such as cabbages and broad and runner beans, which became well integrated into the Indian diet. Punjabi-Muslim food probably suffered the least at the hand of external influences because such curries were already based on meat and were therefore less adapted and altered by the meat-eating foreigners than were vegetarian curries.

European incursions into the subcontinent culminated in the attempted control of the region by the British East India Company and eventual absorption of India within the British Empire. Before this was achieved, however, British disregard for Indian religious beliefs was the catalyst for the Indian Mutiny of 1857. The mutiny was set in motion by the introduction of the new Enfield rifle, the cartridges for which were partially coated with grease and had to be bitten open before loading. Rumours flew through the ranks of the Indian sepoys that the grease was either beef or pork fat. For a caste Hindu to bite on the fat of the sacred cow was an inconceivable sin; to a Muslim, the fat of the unclean pig was insufferable pollution.

The Raj produced some unique Anglo-Indian results, one example of which is Worcestershire sauce. It is one of the few pungent sauces to have survived from its 19th-century heyday and its recipe is a well-guarded secret, containing typically Indian ingredients that include tamarind, shallots, garlic and spices such as cardamom and ginger.

When British rule came to an end in 1947, the subcontinent was partitioned along religious lines into two separate countries – India with a majority of Hindus, and Pakistan with a majority of Muslims. The eastern part of Pakistan later gained independence as Bangladesh. India remains ethnically diverse today, containing the many different religious sects, castes and tribes and major and minor linguistic groups, the existence of which still contribute to the considerable regional variations in Indian cuisine.

REGIONAL DIFFERENCES

Today, people tend to consume two or three meals per day depending on income. The bulk of almost all meals is whatever the regional staple might be – rice throughout most of the east and south, flat wheat bread like chapati in the north and north-west. This is usually supplemented with dhal (a pulse dish), a vegetable dish, possibly a meat dish, a bowl of yogurt or a yogurt relish and a freshly prepared chutney or small, relish-like salad dish.

As a general rule, foods tend to be hotter the further south you go in India. In more detail, the different regions in the country can be characterized as follows.

Northern India

The subtly spiced Punjabi and Kashmiri styles of cooking in northern India owe much to the sophistication of the cooks at the luxurious courts of the Moguls, who came from Persia in the 16th century. The Punjab is particularly famous for its tandoori cooking and for its sweetmeats. The Punjabis tend to consume wheat in preference to rice, while Kashmiri cooking is known for its meat cuisine. Ghee is the most commonly used cooking medium.

Southern India

The south is the stronghold of the Hindus. The Brahmins, monitors of the Hindu faith, taught non-violence, advocated vegetarianism and declared the cow a sacred animal. The staple foods in the south are therefore vegetables and rice. Mustard oil, with its slightly sweet flavour, is the commonly used cooking medium and coconut, coconut milk and tamarind are widely used. Curries from this part of India, which include the fierce vindaloos, are thin and fiery and use plenty of chillies. Curry leaves and mustard seeds are the great southern spices, and fenugreek and roasted pulses provide extra nutrition in the diet.

Eastern India

This region, which encompasses Bengal and Bihar, has good access to rivers and the sea so fish is an important part of the local diet. Mustard oil is again the principal cooking medium and foods are spiced with mustard, cumin, anise and fenugreek seeds. The easterners are particularly well known for their delicious sweetmeats and savouries.

Western India

The cuisine of western India is derived principally from Goa and Bombay. Food from Goa, once colonized by the Portuguese, tends to be hot and spicy and uses a lot of coconut milk, vinegar and tamarind juice. Bombay is famed for its chutneys and pickles, its fruit ice creams and its refreshing cold drinks made with fruit juices and yogurt, known as sharbats.

Central India

The cuisine from central India is dominated by the Mogul influence of the north but it also has certain southern touches and adaptations – for example cashew nuts and coconut have replaced Turkish walnuts and Persian almonds. The Moguls ate beef, unlike the Hindus, and their culinary influence is particularly evident in many regional meat dishes.

savouries
&small dishes

Indians love to snack and can always be seen opening up newspaper cones or unwrapping tea towel bundles of goodies to be nibbled. The best place to eat samosas is undoubtedly right on the street where the odours from a samosa maker are too overwhelming to resist. All kinds of kebabs are also sold at open street stalls. Other popular snacks are grilled cashew nuts and lentil and aubergine fritters served with yogurt sauce or chutney.

Pakora

125 g /4 oz gram flour (besan)
1 teaspoon salt
½ teaspoon chilli powder
about 150 ml/¼ pint water
2 green chillies, finely chopped
1 tablespoon finely chopped fresh
    coriander
1 teaspoon melted butter or ghee
2 onions, cut into rings
oil, for deep-frying
8 small fresh spinach leaves
2–3 potatoes, parboiled and sliced
whole red chillies, fried, to garnish

Pakora comprise onion rings, spinach leaves and parboiled potatoes, which are dipped into a spicy batter and deep-fried until they are crisp and golden.

1 Sift the flour, salt and chilli powder into a bowl. Stir in sufficient water to make a thick batter and beat well until smooth. Leave to stand for 30 minutes.
2 Stir the chillies and fresh coriander into the batter, then add the melted butter or ghee. Drop in the onion rings to coat thickly with batter.
3 Heat the oil in a deep pan to 190°C/375°F, or until a cube of bread browns in 30 seconds. Drop in the onion rings and deep-fry until crisp and golden. Remove from the pan with a slotted spoon, drain on kitchen paper and keep warm.
4 Dip the spinach leaves into the batter and deep-fry in the same way, adding more oil to the pan if necessary.
5 Finally, repeat the process with the potato slices. Serve the pakora hot, garnished with whole fried chillies.

Serves 4
Preparation time: 15 minutes, plus standing
Cooking time: 20 minutes

Cook's Note
Besan, or gram flour, is ground from channa dhal lentils, which come from the chickpea family. (When split and skinned, these lentils are bright yellow and resemble split peas.) Gram flour is often used in Indian cooking instead of wheat flour and is a particularly useful ingredient when cooking for people who are allergic to gluten, a component of all wheat products. It is available in larger supermarkets and Indian grocers.

Spiced Scrambled Eggs

50 g/2 oz butter
1 onion, finely chopped
2 green chillies, finely chopped
8 eggs, lightly beaten with
    2 tablespoons water
1 tablespoon finely chopped
    fresh coriander
salt

Scrambled eggs, flavoured with chillies and coriander.

1 Heat the butter in a large frying pan, add the onion and fry until deep golden. Add the chillies and fry for 30 seconds, then add the beaten eggs, fresh coriander and salt to taste.
2 Cook, stirring, until the eggs are scrambled and set. Serve hot.

Serves 4
Preparation time: 5–10 minutes
Cooking time: 5 minutes

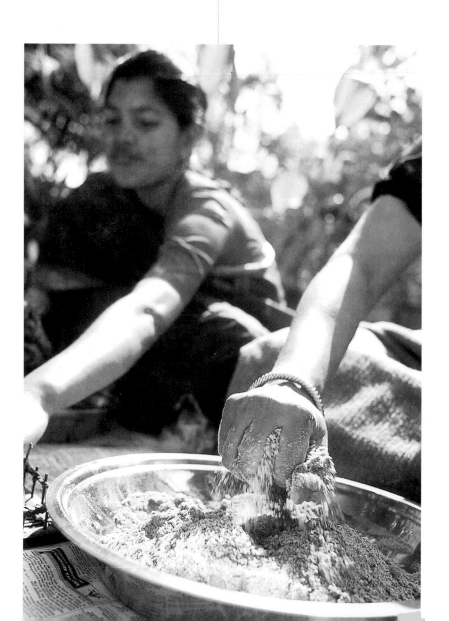

Lamb Kebabs

A combination of minced lamb and flavourings. If liked, these kebabs can be shaped around presoaked wooden skewers and then cooked.

1 Combine all the ingredients together very thoroughly in a large bowl and season with salt and pepper to taste. Using your hands, roll the mixture into 8–12 thin sausage shapes.
2 Place the kebabs under a preheated moderate grill and cook for about 10 minutes, turning several times. Serve garnished with chopped parsley and onion.

Serves 4
Preparation time: 10–15 minutes
Cooking time: 10 minutes

500 g/1 lb minced lamb
2 tablespoons finely chopped
   celery leaves
2 tablespoons chopped parsley
2 onions, finely chopped
1 teaspoon turmeric
salt and pepper
TO GARNISH:
chopped parsley
finely chopped onion

'To light a lamp in the house is like the flowering of the lotus on the lake.'

Proverb

Vegetable Samosas

PASTRY:
125 g/4 oz plain flour
¼ teaspoon salt
25 g/1 oz ghee or butter
2–3 tablespoons water
FILLING:
1 tablespoon vegetable oil
1 teaspoon mustard seeds
1 small onion, finely chopped
2 green chillies, finely chopped
¼ teaspoon turmeric
1 teaspoon finely chopped fresh
    root ginger
125 g/4 oz frozen peas
125 g/4 oz cooked potatoes, diced
½ tablespoon chopped fresh
    coriander
1 tablespoon lemon juice
oil, for deep-frying
salt

1 Sift the flour and salt into a mixing bowl. Rub in the ghee or butter until the mixture resembles breadcrumbs. Add the water and knead to a smooth dough. Cover and chill.
2 Meanwhile, prepare the filling. Heat the oil in a pan and add the mustard seeds. Leave for a few seconds until they start to pop, then add the onion and fry until golden. Add the chillies, turmeric, ginger and salt to taste and fry for 3 minutes. If the mixture sticks to the pan, add ½ tablespoon water and stir. Add the peas, stir and cook for 2 minutes. Add the potatoes and fresh coriander, stir and cook for 1 minute. Stir in the lemon juice and leave to cool slightly.
3 Divide the pastry into 8 pieces. Dust with flour and roll each piece into a thin circle, then cut each circle in half. Fold each semi-circle into a cone and brush the seam with water to seal.
4 Fill the cones with a spoonful of the filling. Dampen the top edge and seal firmly. Heat the oil for deep-frying in a deep pan to 190°C/375°F, or until a cube of bread browns in 30 seconds. Deep-fry the samosas until crisp and golden. Serve hot or warm.

Serves 4
Preparation time: 15 minutes
Cooking time: 35 minutes

Meat Samosas

Samosas are deep-fried pastries stuffed with vegetables or meat, herbs and spices.

1 Sift the flour and salt into a mixing bowl. Rub in the ghee or butter until the mixture resembles breadcrumbs. Add the water and knead thoroughly to a very smooth dough. Cover and chill while preparing the filling.

2 Heat the oil in a pan, add the onion and garlic and fry until golden. Add the chilli and chilli powder and fry for 3 minutes. Stir in the meat and cook until well browned. Add the tomato, chopped fresh coriander and salt to taste and simmer gently for 20 minutes, until the meat is tender and the mixture is dry. Skim off any fat, stir well and leave to cool slightly.

3 Divide the pastry into 8 pieces. Dust with flour and roll each piece into a thin circle, then cut each circle in half. Fold each semi-circle into a cone and brush the seam with water to seal.

4 Fill the cones with a spoonful of the filling, taking care not to overfill them. Dampen the top edge and seal firmly. Heat the oil for deep-frying in a deep pan to 190°C/375°F, or until a cube of bread browns in 30 seconds. Deep-fry the samosas until crisp and golden. Serve hot or warm.

Serves 4
Preparation time: 15 minutes
Cooking time: 35 minutes

PASTRY:
125 g/4 oz plain flour
¼ teaspoon salt
25 g/1 oz ghee or butter
2–3 tablespoons water
FILLING:
1 tablespoon vegetable oil
1 small onion, finely chopped
1 garlic clove, crushed
1 green chilli, finely chopped
½ teaspoon chilli powder
250 g/8 oz minced beef
125 g/4 oz tomato, skinned and chopped
1 tablespoon chopped fresh coriander
oil, for deep-frying
salt

Stuffed Peppers

5 tablespoons vegetable oil
1 onion, finely chopped
2 teaspoons ground coriander
1 teaspoon ground cumin
½ teaspoon chilli powder
375 g/12 oz minced beef
3 tablespoons long-grain rice,
  cooked
4 large green or red peppers
425 g/14 oz can tomatoes
salt
sprigs of fresh coriander, to garnish

1 Heat 3 tablespoons of the oil in a pan, add the onion and fry until golden. Add the spices and cook for 2 minutes. Add the minced beef and fry, stirring, until browned. Add the rice and salt to taste and cook for 2 minutes. Remove from the heat and leave to cool.
2 Slice the peppers lengthways and discard the seeds and cores. Fill the pepper shells with the meat mixture.
3 Heat the remaining oil in a pan just large enough to hold the peppers. Place the peppers in the pan. Pour a little of the canned tomato juice into each pepper and the remaining juice and tomatoes into the pan, seasoning with salt to taste. Bring to simmering point, cover and cook for about 25 minutes, until the peppers are tender. Pour the remaining tomatoes over the peppers and serve, garnished with coriander sprigs.

Serves 4
Preparation time: 10 minutes
Cooking time: 40 minutes

*'The full moon by shedding soft light
helps the buds of the lotus to open.'*

Vyasa

Stuffed Cabbage Leaves

1 cabbage
5 tablespoons vegetable oil
1 onion, chopped
1 cm/½ inch piece fresh root
    ginger, chopped
1 teaspoon turmeric
500 g/1 lb lean minced lamb
75 g/3 oz long-grain rice
2 tomatoes, skinned and chopped
grated rind and juice of 2 lemons
2 teaspoons sugar
150 ml/¼ pint water
salt and pepper

1 Hollow out the stem end of the cabbage with a sharp knife. Place the cabbage in a large pan, cover with water and bring to the boil. Remove from the heat, cover the pan and leave to stand for 15 minutes. Drain.

2 Heat 2 tablespoons of the oil in another pan, add the onion and fry until soft. Add the ginger and turmeric and fry gently for 1 minute. Add the minced lamb and fry briefly until brown. Cool slightly, then stir in the rice, tomatoes, lemon rind and juice and sugar. Mix well and season with salt and pepper to taste.

3 Carefully remove 12 inner leaves from the cabbage. Lay them flat on a work surface and divide the meat mixture between the 12 leaves, gently squeezing out and reserving any liquid. Fold each leaf into a parcel.

4 Heat the remaining oil in a large frying pan. Lay the cabbage rolls in one layer in the pan as close together as possible. Pour over the reserved liquid from the filling and the measured water. Bring to simmering point, cover and cook for about 30 minutes.

5 If the liquid has not evaporated, increase the heat and cook, uncovered, for a few minutes. Lower the heat, turn the rolls, cover and cook for another 5 minutes before serving.

Serves 4–6
Preparation time: 30 minutes
Cooking time: 50–55 minutes

Chilli Fry

1 Heat the oil in a frying pan, add the onion and fry until soft. Add the ground coriander, turmeric, ginger and chilli and fry over a low heat for 5 minutes. If the mixture becomes dry, add 1 tablespoon of water to the pan.

2 Add the strips of steak, increase the heat and cook, stirring, until browned all over. Add the chopped pepper, cover and simmer gently for 5–10 minutes, until the meat is tender. Add the tomatoes, lemon juice and salt to taste and cook, uncovered, for 2–3 minutes – the dish should be rather dry. Serve with lemon wedges.

Serves 4

Preparation time: 15 minutes
Cooking time: 25 minutes

4 tablespoons vegetable oil
I large onion, finely chopped
½ teaspoon ground coriander
½ teaspoon turmeric
2.5 cm/I inch piece fresh root
　ginger, finely chopped
I chilli, chopped
500 g/I lb frying steak, cut into
　strips about 2.5 x I cm/
　I x ½ inch
I green or red pepper, cored,
　deseeded and roughly chopped
2 tomatoes, quartered
4 tablespoons lemon juice
salt
lemon wedges, to serve

Chicken Tikka

150 g/5 oz natural yogurt
1 tablespoon grated fresh
    root ginger
2 garlic cloves, crushed
1 teaspoon chilli powder
1 tablespoon ground coriander
½ teaspoon salt
4 tablespoons lemon juice
2 tablespoons vegetable oil
750 g/1½ lb chicken breasts,
    skinned and boned
TO GARNISH:
lemon or lime wedges, lightly fried
1 red onion, diced

A mild dish made with chicken which is marinated with yogurt, ginger and chilli before being grilled.

1 Mix all the ingredients except the chicken together in a bowl. Cut the chicken into cubes and drop into the marinade. Cover and leave in the refrigerator overnight.
2 Thread the pieces of chicken on to 4 metal or presoaked wooden skewers and cook under a preheated hot grill for 5–6 minutes, turning frequently.
3 The chicken can be left on the skewers or removed and arranged on individual serving plates. Serve garnished with fried lemon or lime wedges and diced red onion.

Serves 4
Preparation time: 10–15 minutes, plus marinating
Cooking time: 5–6 minutes

*'As long as the earth and the sky last,
smile like a flower in the garden of the world.'*

Vali

lamb, beef
& pork

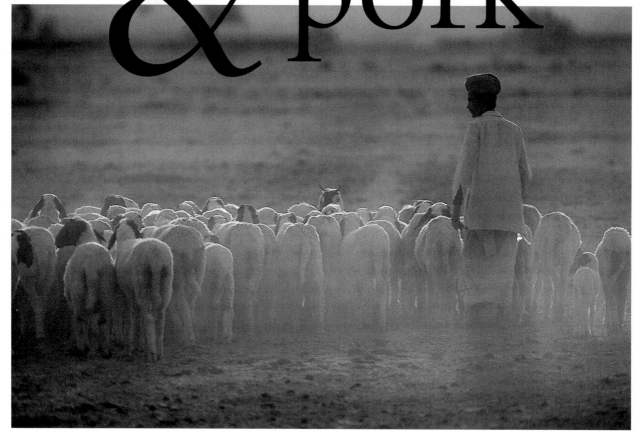

Despite the fact that Indians eat little meat, livestock-raising plays an important role in agriculture and India has by far the largest bovine population of any country in the world. Cattle and buffalo provide milk and a source of meat for those Indians for whom beef-eating is not taboo. The Hindus and Muslims of India do not generally eat pork but Indian Christians do, hence the Goan-style dishes, which often include pork.

Mince with Potatoes and Peas

This is a relatively mild minced beef and vegetable curry.

1 Heat the oil in a frying pan, add the onions and cook until soft. Add the spices and fry for 5 minutes over a low heat. If the mixture starts to burn, add 1 tablespoon of water. Stir in the minced beef and cook over a high heat until very well browned.
2 Meanwhile, bring a saucepan of water to the boil, add the potatoes and salt to taste. Lower the heat, cover and cook gently for 5 minutes, then add the peas. Continue cooking until the potatoes and peas are tender. Drain the potatoes and peas and stir into the mince mixture until well combined. Serve hot.

Serves 4
Preparation time: 10 minutes
Cooking time: 30 minutes

Cook's Note
Garam masala is a dry spice mixture – 'garam' meaning hot and 'masala' meaning spices – which varies from region to region. It may be added during cooking or used as a garnish. Many Indian cooks make up their own favourite blend of spices but it is available ready-made from good supermarkets and Indian grocers.

---

4 tablespoons vegetable oil
2 onions, finely chopped
2 teaspoons ground coriander
½ teaspoon turmeric
2.5 cm/1 inch piece fresh root
   ginger, finely chopped
1 chilli, finely chopped
1 heaped teaspoon garam masala
500 g/1 lb minced beef
250 g/8 oz small potatoes,
   quartered
500 g/1 lb shelled peas
salt

Stuffed Aubergines

2 large aubergines
3 tablespoons vegetable oil
I onion, finely chopped
I garlic clove, finely chopped
2 green chillies, deseeded and
finely chopped
I teaspoon turmeric
500 g/I lb minced beef
I egg, lightly beaten
2–3 tablespoons fresh
breadcrumbs
salt

Aubergines stuffed with minced beef and breadcrumbs and grilled.

1 Cook the whole aubergines in a large pan of salted boiling water for 15 minutes, or until almost tender. Drain thoroughly and leave to cool.
2 Heat the oil in a pan, add the onion and fry until golden. Add the garlic, chillies and turmeric and fry for 2 minutes. Add the mince and cook, stirring, until brown all over. Season with salt to taste and cook gently for 20 minutes, until the meat is tender.
3 Cut the aubergines in half lengthways. Carefully scoop out the flesh. Add it to the meat mixture and mix well. Adjust the seasoning to taste. Fill the aubergine shells with the meat mixture, brush with the beaten egg and cover with breadcrumbs. Place under a preheated moderate grill and cook for 4–5 minutes, until golden.

Serves 4
Preparation time: 15 minutes
Cooking time: 50 minutes

'Patience is the greatest prayer.'

Proverb

Beef Curry with Potatoes

1 Heat the oil in a large pan, add the onions and fry until lightly browned. Add the garlic, chilli powder, cumin, ground coriander and ginger and cook gently for 5 minutes, stirring occasionally. If the mixture becomes dry, add 2 tablespoons of water.

2 Add the cubes of beef and cook, stirring, until browned all over. Add the tomato purée, salt to taste and just enough water to cover the meat, then stir very well. Bring to the boil, cover and simmer for about 1 hour, or until the meat is almost tender. Add the potatoes and whole chillies and simmer until the potatoes are cooked.

Serves 4

Preparation time: 15 minutes
Cooking time: 1¼–1½ hours

4 tablespoons vegetable oil
2 onions, finely chopped
2 garlic cloves, chopped
1 teaspoon chilli powder
1 tablespoon ground cumin
1½ tablespoons ground coriander
2.5 cm/1 inch piece fresh root
 ginger, finely chopped
750 g/1½ lb stewing steak, cubed
2 tablespoons tomato purée
375 g/12 oz small new potatoes
4 green chillies
salt

Beef with Coconut Milk

3 tablespoons vegetable oil
2 onions, sliced
2 garlic cloves, finely chopped
3 green chillies, chopped
3.5 cm/1½ inch piece fresh root
    ginger, chopped
750 g/1½ lb braising steak, cubed
½ teaspoon chilli powder
1 teaspoon turmeric
1 teaspoon pepper
1 teaspoon ground cumin
½ teaspoon cinnamon
½ teaspoon ground cloves
300 ml/½ pint coconut milk
150 ml/¼ pint vinegar
salt
2 yellow or green chillies, diced,
    to garnish

Cubed braising steak is cooked slowly with a subtle combination of spices and coconut milk, until the meat is tender and succulent and the sauce is rich and thick.

1 Heat the oil in a large pan, add the onions and fry until they are just beginning to brown, then add the garlic, chillies and ginger. Fry for 1 minute, then add the beef and remaining spices. Stir well and cook for 5 minutes, stirring occasionally.
2 Add the coconut milk, which should just cover the meat; if it does not, add a little water. Add salt to taste. Bring to simmering point, cover and cook for about 1½ hours, until the meat is almost tender.
3 Add the vinegar and continue cooking for about 30 minutes, until the meat is tender and the gravy is thick. Serve garnished with diced chillies.

Serves 4
Preparation time: 20 minutes
Cooking time: 2–2¼ hours

Cook's Note
Instead of coconut milk in this recipe you could use 75 g/3 oz creamed coconut, melted in 250 ml/8 fl oz warm water. Creamed coconut is sold in blocks, which should always be softened in warm water before use.

Lamb and Pepper Kebabs

300 g/10 oz natural yogurt
1 tablespoon ground coriander
½ teaspoon chilli powder
1 tablespoon vegetable oil
750 g/1½ lb boned leg of
    lamb, cubed
4 onions
8 tomatoes
2 red peppers, cored, deseeded
    and cut into squares
salt
2 tablespoons finely chopped fresh
    coriander, to garnish

1 Put the yogurt, ground coriander, chilli powder, oil and salt to taste in a large bowl and stir to combine. Add the lamb, mix well, cover and leave in the refrigerator overnight.

2 Cut the onions into quarters and separate the layers. Cut the tomatoes in half.

3 Thread the pieces of onion, lamb and red pepper alternately on to 8 metal or presoaked wooden skewers, beginning and ending each kebab with a tomato half. Place under a preheated hot grill and cook for about 10 minutes, turning frequently and basting with any remaining marinade as necessary. Sprinkle with the chopped fresh coriander before serving.

Serves 4
Preparation time: 15 minutes, plus marinating
Cooking time: 10 minutes

'To live a pure unselfish life, one must count nothing as one's own in the midst of abundance.'

Buddha

Pork Vindaloo

This hot curry owes some of its kick to the combination of spices, including mustard seeds, and the addition of vinegar.

1 Mix the spices and a little salt with the vinegar. Put the onion, garlic and pork into a bowl. Pour over the vinegar mixture, cover and leave in the refrigerator overnight.

2 Heat the oil in a large pan, add the pork mixture and bring to simmering point. Cover and cook for about 45 minutes, or until the pork is tender.

Serves 4
Preparation time: 10 minutes, plus marinating
Cooking time: 50 minutes

1–2 teaspoons chilli powder
1 teaspoon turmeric
2 teaspoons ground cumin
2 teaspoons ground mustard seeds
2 tablespoons ground coriander
3.5 cm/1½ inch piece fresh root
    ginger, finely chopped
150 ml/¼ pint vinegar
1 large onion, finely chopped
2 garlic cloves, crushed
750 g/1½ lb pork fillet, cubed
4 tablespoons vegetable oil
salt

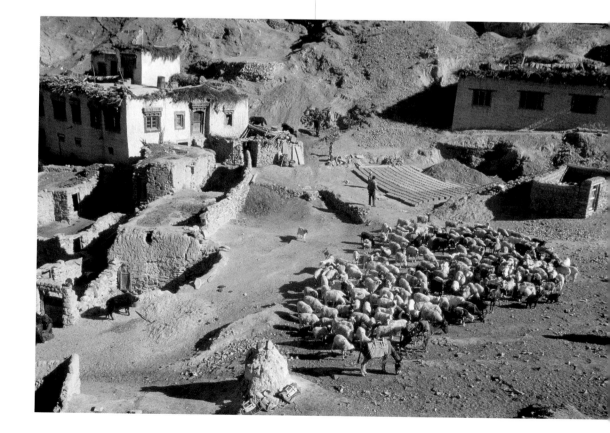

Spiced Roast Lamb

2.5 kg/5 lb leg of lamb, skin and fat removed
50 g/2 oz fresh root ginger, chopped
6 garlic cloves
grated rind of 1 lemon
8 tablespoons lemon juice
2 teaspoons cumin seeds
6 cardamom pods, peeled
1 teaspoon ground cloves
1 teaspoon turmeric
1½ teaspoons chilli powder
1 tablespoon salt
300 g/10 oz natural yogurt
150 g/5 oz whole unpeeled almonds
4 tablespoons brown sugar
1 teaspoon saffron threads, infused in 3 tablespoons boiling water
Saffron Rice, to serve
    (see page 114)

A leg of lamb that is coated in a mixture of spices and cooked slowly to allow the flavours to fully develop.

1 Prick the lamb all over with a fork and make about 12 deep cuts in the meat.
2 Blend the ginger, garlic, lemon rind and juice, spices and salt in a blender or food processor. Spread the paste over the lamb and leave to stand for 1 hour in a flameproof casserole.
3 Blend 4 tablespoons of the natural yogurt with the almonds and 2 tablespoons of the sugar in a blender or food processor. Stir in the remaining yogurt and pour over the lamb. Cover the casserole tightly and leave for 48 hours in the refrigerator.
4 Let the meat return to room temperature. Sprinkle over the remaining sugar and cook, uncovered, in a preheated oven, 220°C/425°F/Gas Mark 7, for 30 minutes. Cover, reduce the temperature to 160°C/325°F/Gas Mark 3 and cook for 3 hours, basting occasionally. Sprinkle the saffron water over the meat and cook for a further 30 minutes, or until very tender.
5 Remove the meat from the casserole, wrap it in foil and keep warm. Skim off the fat from the liquid in the casserole and boil the sauce until thick. Place the meat on a warmed dish and pour over the sauce. Carve into thick slices and serve with Saffron Rice.

Serves 6
Preparation time: 20 minutes, plus standing and marinating
Cooking time: 4 hours
Oven temperature: 220°C/425°F/Gas Mark 7, then 160°C/325°F/Gas Mark 3

Dry Pork Curry

750 g/1½ lb pork fillets
2 tablespoons coriander seeds,
    roughly pounded with a pestle
    and mortar
1 teaspoon pepper
1 tablespoon paprika
4 tablespoons vegetable oil
salt
2 tablespoons finely chopped fresh
    coriander, to garnish (optional)
tomato and red onion salad,
    to serve

1 Slit the pork fillets lengthways and cut each half into quarters. Prick the pieces all over with a fork. Mix together the coriander seeds, pepper, paprika and salt to taste and rub into the meat on both sides. Leave to stand for 1 hour.
2 Heat the oil in a pan, add the meat and fry quickly on both sides to seal. Reduce the heat and sauté for 5 minutes or until cooked through, stirring and turning to prevent burning.
3 Sprinkle with the fresh coriander, if liked, and serve with a tomato and red onion salad.

Serves 4
Preparation time: 10–15 minutes, plus standing
Cooking time: 10 minutes

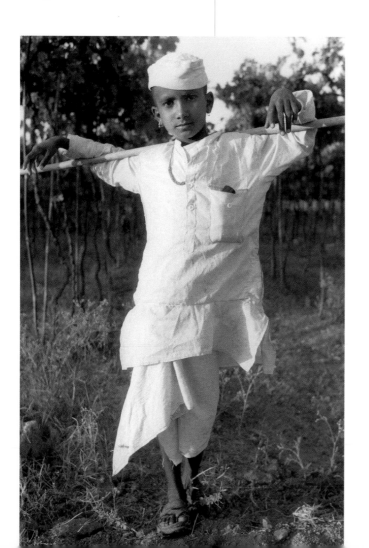

Lamb with Almonds

This is a delicious combination of cubed lamb gently cooked in mildly spiced yogurt with flaked almonds.

1 Heat 2 tablespoons of the oil in a pan, add 1 chopped onion and fry until golden. Add the lamb and 175 g/6 oz of the yogurt. Stir well, cover and simmer for 20 minutes.
2 Place the garlic, ginger, green chillies, coriander seeds, cumin seeds, mint, fresh coriander and 2–3 tablespoons yogurt in a blender or food processor and blend to a paste.
3 Heat the remaining oil in a large pan, add the cardamoms, cloves and cinnamon stick and fry for 1 minute, stirring. Add the second chopped onion and the prepared paste and fry for 5 minutes, stirring constantly.
4 Add the lamb and yogurt mixture, add salt to taste, stir well and bring to simmering point. Cover and cook for 30 minutes. Add the almonds and cook for a further 15 minutes, until the meat is tender. Serve garnished with flaked almonds.

Serves 4
Preparation time: 10–15 minutes
Cooking time: 1¼ hours

4 tablespoons vegetable oil
2 onions, finely chopped
750 g/1½ lb boned leg of lamb, cubed
250 g/8 oz natural yogurt
2 garlic cloves
2.5 cm/1 inch piece fresh root ginger
2 green chillies
1 tablespoon coriander seeds
1 teaspoon cumin seeds
1 teaspoon chopped fresh mint leaves
1 teaspoon chopped fresh coriander
6 cardamom pods
6 cloves
2.5 cm/1 inch piece cinnamon stick
125 g/4 oz flaked almonds, plus extra to garnish
salt

'In this world, everlasting joy lies in observing the laws of nature.'

Iqual

Lamb Korma

750 g/1½ lb boneless leg of lamb,
 cubed
150 g/5 oz natural yogurt
½ teaspoon saffron threads, infused
 in 2 tablespoons boiling water
 for 10 minutes
1 teaspoon salt
2 tablespoons ghee
¼ teaspoon ground cardamom
½ teaspoon cinnamon
1½ teaspoons ground cumin
1½ teaspoons ground coriander
300 ml/½ pint coconut milk
2 tablespoons chopped fresh
 coriander
½ teaspoon caster sugar
BLENDED MIXTURE:
2 onions, chopped
3 garlic cloves, chopped
2.5 cm/1 inch piece fresh root
 ginger, chopped
2 green chillies, deseeded and
 chopped
50 g/2 oz ground almonds
150 ml/¼ pint water
TO GARNISH:
fresh coriander leaves
25 g/1 oz flaked almonds, toasted

A favourite mild lamb curry cooked with yogurt, coconut milk, saffron and ground almonds.

1 Place the pieces of lamb in a bowl. Mix together the yogurt, saffron and its water and the salt. Pour over the lamb, cover and leave to marinate for 2 hours.
2 Place the ingredients for the blended mixture in a blender or food processor and blend to a thick paste. Set aside.
3 Heat the ghee in a pan, add the ground cardamom, cinnamon, cumin and ground coriander and cook over a gentle heat for 1 minute. Stir in the blended paste and cook, stirring frequently, for a further 5 minutes.
4 Add the coconut milk and the lamb and saffron yogurt, bring to the boil, then lower the heat. Cover the pan and cook very gently, stirring occasionally, for 45 minutes, or until the lamb is tender and the sauce is thick.
5 Stir in the chopped fresh coriander and the caster sugar and serve hot, garnished with coriander leaves and toasted flaked almonds.

Serves 4–6
Preparation time: 25 minutes, plus marinating
Cooking time: 1 hour

Cook's Note
Ghee is a type of clarified butter, which is made by heating ordinary butter to remove the milk solids. It has a higher burning point than most other oils and is therefore ideal for frying delicate foods. Vegetable ghee is readily available and is a healthier alternative to standard ghee, with a slightly different flavour and texture. Vegetable oil is an acceptable substitute.

Kashmiri Kofta Curry

A fragrant meatball curry that goes well with Indian bread such as Naan (see page 122).

1 To make the lamb meatballs, place the lamb, ginger, red chilli, fresh coriander, 1 teaspoon of the garam masala, 1 teaspoon of the salt and the pepper in a bowl. Mix thoroughly, then divide the mixture into 16 and shape each portion into a small meatball.
2 Heat the oil in a heavy-based frying pan, add the meatballs and fry over a gentle heat for 5 minutes, turning occasionally to seal them. Using a slotted spoon, transfer the meatballs to a saucepan.
3 In a jug, mix together the yogurt, sugar, chilli powder, the remaining garam masala and salt and the water. Pour the yogurt mixture over the meatballs, then cook the curry, uncovered, over a medium heat for 10 minutes, or until the meatballs are cooked and most of the liquid has been absorbed, leaving just a little sauce.
4 Serve hot, garnished with ground cardamom and coriander sprigs.

Serves 4
Preparation time: 20 minutes
Cooking time: 20 minutes

500 g/1 lb lean minced lamb
1 tablespoon grated fresh root ginger
1 large red chilli, deseeded and very finely chopped
2 tablespoons chopped fresh coriander
1 tablespoon garam masala
1½ teaspoons salt
¼ teaspoon pepper
3 tablespoons vegetable oil
150 g/5 oz natural yogurt
1 teaspoon soft brown sugar
½ teaspoon chilli powder
300 ml/½ pint water
TO GARNISH:
pinch of ground cardamom
sprigs of fresh coriander

Goan Lamb and Pork Curry

3 tablespoons vegetable oil
2 onions, finely chopped
3 garlic cloves, crushed
1 tablespoon grated fresh root
   ginger
2 large red chillies, quartered
   lengthways and deseeded
375 g/12 oz lamb fillet, cut into
   bite-sized pieces
375 g/12 oz lean pork, cut into
   bite-sized pieces
1 teaspoon salt
150 ml/¼ pint water
75 ml/3 fl oz distilled malt vinegar
1 green and 1 red chilli, cut into
   rings, to garnish
Saffron Rice, to serve
   (see page 114)
SPICE MIXTURE:
1 teaspoon ground cumin
1 teaspoon ground coriander
1 teaspoon chilli powder
1 tablespoon black mustard seeds
1 tablespoon nigella seeds (kalonji)
1 tablespoon garam masala

An unusual curry from Goa in which two types of meat are cooked together.

1 Heat the oil in a heavy-based pan, add the onions, garlic, ginger and chillies and cook over a low heat, stirring frequently, for about 5 minutes, until softened.
2 Place the ingredients for the spice mixture in an electric spice mill or use a pestle and mortar and grind to produce a fine powder. Add the ground spices to the pan and fry for a further 1 minute.
3 Add the pieces of lamb and pork to the pan, together with the salt. Coat the meat in the spices and cook for 2 minutes. Add the water and the vinegar to the pan and stir well to combine the ingredients. Cover and simmer over a gentle heat, stirring occasionally, for about 45 minutes, or until the meat is tender.
4 Remove the lid, increase the heat and cook for a further 15 minutes, stirring frequently, until the sauce is thick and dark. Taste and adjust the seasoning if necessary.
5 Transfer the curry to a warmed serving dish and garnish with chilli rings. Serve with Saffron Rice.

Serves 6
Preparation time: 15–20 minutes
Cooking time: 1¼ hours

Lamb Tikka Masala

750 g/1½ lb lean lamb, cubed
1 quantity Tandoori Marinade
    (see page 56)
MASALA SAUCE:
4 tablespoons ghee
1 quantity Curry Purée
    (see page 48)
1 tablespoon tandoori paste
2 teaspoons tomato purée
2 tomatoes, skinned and chopped
1 red pepper, cored, deseeded and
    puréed
1 tablespoon chopped fresh
    coriander
1 tablespoon ground almonds
2 tablespoons single cream
white sugar, to taste
salt
TO GARNISH:
lime slices, quartered
sprigs of parsley

Cubes of lamb are marinated in a tandoori marinade, then cooked on skewers and added to a masala sauce.

1 Combine the lamb and tandoori marinade in a bowl. Cover and leave in the refrigerator for about 24 hours.
2 Remove the pieces of lamb from the marinade, reserving the marinade. Thread the pieces of lamb on to 4 metal or presoaked wooden skewers and and cook under a preheated moderate grill for 15–20 minutes, turning them once halfway through the cooking time.
3 Meanwhile, make the masala sauce. Heat the ghee in a large frying pan or wok. Stir-fry the curry purée for 5 minutes. Add the tandoori paste and the reserved marinade and stir-fry for 2 minutes. Add the tomato purée, chopped tomatoes and puréed red pepper. Bring to simmering point and add a little water, if necessary, to achieve a creamy textured sauce. Add the fresh coriander, ground almonds, cream and sugar and salt to taste.
4 When the lamb tikkas are cooked, remove them from the skewers and stir them into the masala sauce. Serve garnished with lime slices and parsley.

Serves 4
Preparation time: 30 minutes, plus marinating
Cooking time: 25–30 minutes

Spicy Beef Curry

Marinated beef cooked with milk, almonds and coconut.

1 Slice the beef into 4 steaks. Beat with a rolling pin or the back of a wooden spoon until they are 5 mm/¼ inch thick. Cut each steak in half to give 8 pieces. Place the steaks in a non-metallic dish. Add the red wine and spices and leave to marinate in the refrigerator for up to 24 hours.

2 Heat the oil in a frying pan or wok and stir-fry the curry purée for 5 minutes. Add the curry paste and mix well. Lift the steaks out of the marinade and add to the pan 2 at a time. Fry the steaks quickly to seal – allowing about 20 seconds on each side. When all the steaks are in the pan and are brown, add the milk, ground almonds, coconut and the marinade. Simmer for 10 minutes, until the meat is cooked.

3 Transfer to a warmed serving dish and pour the cream over the top. Garnish with parsley and pistachio nuts and serve with rice.

Serves 4
Preparation time: 20 minutes, plus marinating
Cooking time: 15–20 minutes

Cook's Note
Curry pastes are available in different strengths and flavours. A curry paste is simply a 'wet' blend of spices – as opposed to a 'dry' blend such as garam masala – cooked with oil and vinegar, which help to preserve them.

750 g/1½ lb lean beef rump, fillet
   or topside
150 ml/¼ pint red wine
4 tablespoons vegetable oil
1 quantity Curry Purée
   (see page 48)
1 tablespoon mild curry paste
175 ml/6 fl oz milk
2 tablespoons ground almonds
2 tablespoons desiccated coconut
4 tablespoons double cream
salt
SPICES:
2 teaspoons garam masala
1 teaspoon mace
½ teaspoon cinnamon
TO GARNISH:
sprigs of parsley
chopped pistachio nuts
steamed or boiled rice, to serve

Lamb and Vegetable Curry

50 g/2 oz lentils
50 g/2 oz chickpeas
50 g/2 oz moong dhal
750 g/1½ lb lamb fillet, cut into
    5 cm/2 inch cubes
3 tablespoons ghee
1 large onion, thinly sliced
2 tablespoons tomato purée
300 ml/½ pint water
salt and pepper
TO GARNISH:
sprigs of fresh coriander
deep-fried onion rings
red chillies, cut into rings
boiled rice or Saffron Rice,
    to serve (see page 114)
VEGETABLES:
300 g/10 oz aubergine, cubed
250 g/8 oz pumpkin, peeled and
    cubed
125 g/4 oz potato, peeled and
    cubed
2 onions, roughly chopped
2 tomatoes, skinned and chopped
75 g/3 oz fresh spinach, washed
MASALA MIXTURE:
3 red chillies, deseeded and
    chopped
3 green chillies, deseeded and
    chopped
6 garlic cloves, crushed
2.5 cm/1 inch piece fresh root
    ginger, finely chopped
25 g/1 oz fresh coriander leaves
15 g/½ oz mint leaves
4 tablespoons water
DRY SPICE MIXTURE:
2 teaspoons turmeric
1 teaspoon black mustard seeds
½ teaspoon cinnamon
¼ teaspoon fenugreek powder
2 tablespoons dhana jeera powder
4 cardamom pods, crushed

A spicy curry that is cooked with lentils in masala and a dry spice mixture.

1 Wash the lentils, chickpeas and moong dhal in several changes of cold water and leave them to soak overnight in a large bowl of cold water.

2 The next day, drain the pulses and place them in a large pan with the cubed lamb. Pour over enough boiling water to cover and season generously with salt. Bring to the boil, skim any scum from the surface, then cover and simmer the pulses and meat, stirring occasionally, for about 20 minutes.

3 Add all the prepared vegetables to the pan, stir well and continue cooking for a further 40 minutes, until the pulses and vegetables are cooked and the lamb is tender. Drain the liquid from the pan and remove the pieces of meat using a slotted spoon. Set the meat aside and tip the cooked vegetables and pulses into a blender or food processor. Blend to produce a thick purée. Tip into a bowl and set aside.

4 Heat the ghee in a large, heavy-based frying pan and fry the thinly sliced onion over a gentle heat for 5 minutes, until softened and golden.

5 Place all the ingredients for the masala mixture in the blender or food processor and blend to a paste. Add this paste to the softened onion in the frying pan and cook over a low heat for a further 3 minutes. Stir in the dry spice mixture and cook, stirring constantly, for 3 minutes, until the mixture is aromatic.

6 Add the pieces of lamb and the pulse and vegetable purée to the pan, together with the tomato purée and water. Season with salt and pepper, cover and simmer the curry for about 30 minutes until it is thick. If it becomes too dry during cooking, add a little more water to the pan. Taste and adjust the seasoning if necessary.

7 Transfer the curry to a warmed serving dish. Garnish with coriander sprigs, deep-fried onion rings and chilli rings and serve immediately with boiled rice or Saffron Rice.

Serves 6
Preparation time: 40 minutes, plus soaking
Cooking time: 1¾ hours

Beef with Fenugreek

4 tablespoons ghee
2 tablespoons mild curry paste
750 g/1½ lb stewing beef, cubed
4 tomatoes, chopped
4 tablespoons dried fenugreek
  leaves (methi)
1 tablespoon garam masala
salt
2 tablespoons chopped parsley,
  to garnish
CURRY PURÉE:
6 tablespoons ghee
2–4 garlic cloves, finely chopped
5 cm/2 inch piece fresh root
  ginger, finely chopped
½ onion, finely chopped
2 teaspoons mild curry paste
1 teaspoon tomato purée
1 tablespoon chopped fresh
  coriander

Cubes of beef cooked with dried fenugreek leaves produce this moist savoury curry.

1 To make the curry purée, heat the ghee in a large frying pan or wok. Stir-fry the garlic for 1 minute. Add the ginger and stir-fry for 1 more minute. Add the onion and stir-fry for 2–3 minutes more. Stir in the curry paste, tomato purée and fresh coriander with enough water to prevent the mixture from sticking. Simmer for 5 minutes.

2 Heat the ghee in another large frying pan or wok and stir-fry the curry purée for 5 minutes. Stir the curry paste in well to blend and add the cubes of beef. Stir-fry for about 5 minutes more to seal the meat.

3 Transfer the meat and sauce to a heavy lidded casserole and bake in a preheated oven, 190°C/375°F/Gas Mark 5, for 20 minutes. Stir in the tomatoes, dried fenugreek, garam masala and salt to taste, with a little water to moisten if necessary. Continue cooking for a further 25 minutes. If at the end of the cooking time there is an excess of oil, spoon it off before serving. Garnish with chopped parsley.

Serves 4
Preparation time: 15 minutes
Cooking time: 1 hour 10 minutes
Oven temperature: 190°C/375°F/Gas Mark 5

Cook's Note
Fenugreek leaves, called 'methi', are widely used, fresh or dried, in Indian cooking. The plant is rich in protein, minerals and vitamins, which makes it an important ingredient in vegetable and dhal dishes eaten in the poorer areas of India.

'If you beat spice it will smell the sweeter.'

Proverb

Beef and Mango Curry

This Nepalese recipe combines stewing beef with a pickle base and fresh mango.

1 Heat the ghee in a large frying pan or wok and stir-fry the curry purée for 5 minutes. Stir in the curry paste and the meat, combining the ingredients well. Continue frying until the meat is sealed – about 5 minutes.
2 Transfer to a heavy lidded casserole and place in a preheated oven, 190°C/375°F/Gas Mark 5, for 20 minutes.
3 Meanwhile, scoop all the flesh from the mango. Place it in a blender or food processor and work to a purée. Add it to the casserole with the chopped pickle, fresh coriander and salt to taste, with a little water to moisten if necessary.
4 Return the casserole to the oven for a further 25 minutes. At the end of the cooking time, spoon off any excess oil before serving. Garnish with fresh mango slices and sprigs of parsley.

Serves 4
Preparation time: 10 minutes
Cooking time: 55 minutes
Oven temperature: 190°C/375°F/Gas Mark 5

4 tablespoons ghee
I quantity Curry Purée
    (see page 48)
I tablespoon mild curry paste
750 g/I½ lb stewing beef, cubed
I fresh mango
3 tablespoons mild mango or
    brinjal pickle, finely chopped
I tablespoon chopped fresh
    coriander
salt
TO GARNISH:
fresh mango slices
sprigs of parsley

Goan Vindaloo

750 g/1½ lb pork fillet or
    tenderloin, cubed
200 ml/7 fl oz vinegar
2–6 teaspoons chilli powder
4 tablespoons ghee
1 quantity Curry Purée
    (see page 48)
4–8 fresh or dried red chillies
salt
sprigs of basil, to garnish
SPICES:
(DRY-ROASTED AND GROUND)
2 teaspoons coriander seeds
1 teaspoon white cumin seeds
10 cm/4 inch piece cinnamon stick
12 cloves
12 green cardamom pods
2 teaspoons black pepper

A hot pork curry cooked with dry-roasted spices, chilli powder and chillies.

1 Place the pork in a non-metallic dish with the vinegar and a quantity of chilli powder according to your taste. Cover and refrigerate for 24 hours.
2 Mix the dry-roasted and ground spices with enough water to make a paste. Heat the ghee in a large frying pan or wok and stir-fry the curry purée for 5 minutes. Add the spice paste, stir-frying for 2 minutes more. Lift the pieces of pork out of the marinade, reserving the liquid, and combine them with the ingredients in the frying pan.
3 Transfer the mixture to a heavy-lidded casserole and bake in a preheated oven, 190°C/375°F/Gas Mark 5, for 1 hour, adding the red chillies to taste after 20 minutes of cooking time, with a little salt and some marinade to moisten if necessary. If at the end of the cooking time there is an excess of oil, spoon it off before serving. Garnish with sprigs of basil.

Serves 4
Preparation time: 15 minutes, plus marinating
Cooking time: 1½ hours
Oven temperature: 190°C/375°F/Gas Mark 5

Cook's Note
Dry-frying spices brings out a more intense flavour. Place them whole in a heavy-based dry frying pan and shake the pan over a fairly high heat for 1–2 minutes. Cool slightly, then grind the dry-roasted spices to a powder using an electric spice mill or a pestle and mortar.

Lamb with Yogurt

Cubed lamb, cooked with yogurt, ginger and dry-roasted cumin seeds.

1 Melt the ghee in a heavy-based frying pan or wok and fry half the onions over a very low heat, until soft and golden brown. Remove from the pan with a slotted spoon and set aside.
2 Increase the heat, add the meat and sauté until it is sealed on all sides. Remove the meat from the pan and set aside.
3 Add the chilli powder, ginger, salt and the remaining onions to the pan, then stir in the yogurt. Cook for 2 minutes, then return the meat to the pan. Cover and simmer for 10 minutes.
4 Add the garlic, cardamom seeds, garam masala, ground cumin seeds and the browned onions. Cover and simmer for 30 minutes, or until the lamb is tender, adding a little water if necessary to prevent it from sticking to the bottom of the wok. Serve hot.

Serves 4
Preparation time: 15–20 minutes
Cooking time: 50 minutes

125 g/4 oz ghee
500 g/1 lb onions, sliced
500 g/1 lb boned shoulder of lamb,
    cut into 2.5 cm/1 inch cubes
1 teaspoon chilli powder
½ teaspoon ground ginger
1 teaspoon salt
300 g/10 oz natural yogurt
2 garlic cloves, crushed
4 cardamom seeds
1 teaspoon garam masala
½ teaspoon cumin seeds,
    dry-roasted and ground
    (see page 50)

Balti Beef *pictured*

4 tablespoons vegetable oil
1 large onion, chopped
½ teaspoon ground coriander
½ teaspoon turmeric
2.5 cm/1 inch piece fresh root
    ginger, finely chopped
1 garlic clove, crushed
1 red chilli, chopped
1 yellow chilli, chopped
500 g/1 lb frying steak, cut into
    strips about 2.5 x 4 cm/
    1 x 1¾ inches
1 green or red pepper, cored,
    deseeded and roughly chopped
2 tomatoes, quartered
4 tablespoons lemon juice
salt
fresh coriander leaves, to garnish

1 Heat the oil in a heavy-based frying pan or wok, add the onion and fry until soft. Add the ground coriander, turmeric, ginger, garlic and chilli and stir-fry over a low heat for 5 minutes. If the mixture becomes dry, add 1 tablespoon of water.
2 Add the steak, increase the heat and stir-fry until browned all over. Add the chopped pepper, then cover and cook over a low heat for 5–10 minutes, stirring occasionally, until the meat is tender. Add the tomatoes, lemon juice and salt to taste and cook, uncovered, for 2–3 minutes. Serve hot, garnished with fresh coriander.

Serves 2–3
Preparation time: 20 minutes
Cooking time: 25 minutes

Calcutta Beef Curry

1 teaspoon salt
1 tablespoon chilli powder
2 teaspoons ground coriander
1 teaspoon pepper
1½ teaspoons turmeric
1 teaspoon ground cumin
1 litre/1¾ pints milk
1–1.25 kg/2–2½ lb braising steak,
    trimmed and cut into
    4 cm/1¾ inch cubes
50 g/2 oz ghee
2 large onions, thinly sliced
5 garlic cloves, thinly sliced
7 cm/3 inch piece fresh root
    ginger, thinly sliced
2 teaspoons garam masala

This rich and hearty curry consists of beef simmered for a long time in a mixture of milk and spices until the meat is tender and the sauce reduced.

1 Put the salt, chilli powder, ground coriander, pepper, turmeric and cumin into a large bowl. Mix in a little of the milk to make a paste, then gradually stir in the remaining milk. Add the cubes of beef and stir well until the beef is evenly coated.
2 Melt the ghee in a heavy-based frying pan or wok, add the onions, garlic and ginger and fry gently for 4–5 minutes, until soft.
3 Remove the beef from the milk and spice mixture with a slotted spoon, add to the pan and stir-fry over a moderate heat until browned on all sides.
4 Increase the heat, add the milk and spice mixture and bring to the boil. Cover the pan, lower the heat and cook gently for 1½–2 hours, or until the beef is tender and the sauce reduced.
5 Just before serving, sprinkle in the garam masala. Increase the heat and boil off any excess liquid to leave a thick sauce. Transfer to a warmed serving dish and serve immediately.

Serves 4–6
Preparation time: 15 minutes
Cooking time: about 2 hours

chicken

In Indian cooking, the skin of the chicken is almost always removed before cooking. This allows the flavour of the spices to penetrate the chicken much better, as well as making the entire dish less fatty. Chicken is often marinated and grilled – as in chicken tikka and chicken tandoori – or stewed with spices, and there are innumerable chicken curry dishes.

Chicken Tikka Masala

750 g/1½ lb skinless, boneless
  chicken breasts, cubed
9–12 tablespoons fresh lemon juice
  or 6 tablespoons bottled
  lemon juice
MASALA SAUCE:
4 tablespoons ghee
1 quantity Curry Purée
  (see page 48)
1 tablespoon tandoori paste
2 teaspoons tomato purée
2 tomatoes, skinned and chopped
1 red pepper, cored, deseeded
  and puréed
1 tablespoon chopped
  fresh coriander
1 tablespoon ground almonds
2 tablespoons single cream
white sugar, to taste
salt
TANDOORI MARINADE:
75 g/3 oz natural yogurt
75 ml/3 fl oz milk
2 tablespoons tandoori masala
1 tablespoon mild curry powder
  or paste
2 teaspoons garam masala
½–2 teaspoons chilli powder
1 tablespoon chopped mint
1 tablespoon chopped fresh
  coriander
2 teaspoons garlic purée
2.5 cm/1 inch piece fresh root
  ginger, finely chopped
1 teaspoon white cumin seeds,
  dry-roasted and ground
  (see page 50)
2 tablespoons lemon juice
TO GARNISH:
diced tomato
sprigs of fresh coriander, chopped

1 Place the chicken in a large bowl and add the lemon juice, working it in with your fingers to 'de-grease' the chicken in preparation for the marinade. Leave to stand for 1 hour.
2 Combine the ingredients for the tandoori marinade in another large bowl, setting aside 2 tablespoons of the marinade to use later. Strain off and discard the juices from the chicken, then add the chicken to the marinade and stir well. Cover and refrigerate for a minimum of 6 hours, or overnight, but preferably for 24 hours.
3 Remove the pieces of chicken, from the marinade and thread on to metal or presoaked wooden skewers and place them under a preheated moderate grill for 10–15 minutes, turning them 2 or 3 times. (Alternatively, the tikkas can be baked in a preheated oven, 190°C/375°F/Gas Mark 5, or stir-fried, without oil, for about 15 minutes in each case.)
4 Meanwhile, make the masala sauce. Heat the ghee in a large frying pan or wok. Stir-fry the curry purée for 5 minutes. Add the tandoori paste and reserved marinade and stir-fry for 2 minutes. Add the tomato purée, tomatoes and puréed red pepper. Bring to simmering point and add a little water if necessary, to achieve a creamy textured sauce. Add the fresh coriander, ground almonds, cream and sugar and salt to taste.
5 When the tikkas are cooked, remove them from the skewers, if using, and stir them into the sauce. Garnish with diced tomato and chopped fresh coriander and serve.

Serves 4
Preparation time: 30 minutes, plus standing and marinating
Cooking time: 20–25 minutes
Oven temperature: 190°C/325°F/Gas Mark 5

Chicken Korma

2 onions
2 garlic cloves
2.5 cm/1 inch piece fresh root ginger, chopped
2 green chillies, chopped
1 tablespoon coriander seeds
1 teaspoon salt
2 tablespoons water
50 g/2 oz almonds
750 g/1½ lb chicken pieces, skinned
3 tablespoons vegetable oil
6 cardamom pods
6 cloves
2.5 cm/1 inch piece cinnamon stick
150 g/5 oz natural yogurt
150 ml/¼ pint single cream
¼ teaspoon powdered saffron, infused in 1 tablespoon warm water
2 tablespoons chopped fresh coriander, to garnish

1 Chop 1 onion and place in a blender or food processor with the garlic, ginger, chillies, coriander seeds, salt, water and half the almonds. Blend until smooth. Place the pieces of chicken in a non-metallic dish. Spoon the mixture over them, mix well and set aside for 1 hour.

2 Finely chop the second onion. Heat the oil in a pan, add the onion, cardamoms, cloves and cinnamon and fry until the onion is soft. Add the chicken and marinade and fry, stirring, until dry.

3 Add the yogurt, a tablespoon at a time, stirring until absorbed. Cover the pan and leave to simmer very gently for 30 minutes, adding a little water if necessary.

4 Place the remaining almonds, the cream and saffron with its infused water in a blender or food processor and blend until smooth. Stir into the chicken and check the seasoning. Cover and simmer for about 5 more minutes, until the chicken is tender.

5 Serve garnished with chopped fresh coriander.

Serves 4
Preparation time: 15 minutes, plus marinating
Cooking time: 45–50 minutes

'Only mad dogs and Englishmen go out in the noonday sun'.

Proverb

Chicken Jalfrezi

1 Heat the ghee in a large frying pan or wok. Stir-fry the cumin and mustard seeds for 1 minute. Add the garlic and stir-fry for 1 minute more. Add the ginger and stir-fry for 2 minutes. Add the sliced onion and stir-fry until golden – about 5 minutes.

2 Combine the chicken pieces with the ingredients in the pan, stirring and turning for 5 more minutes. Add all the remaining ingredients and stir-fry for about 10 more minutes, until cooked through and tender. Serve immediately.

Serves 4

Preparation time: 20 minutes
Cooking time: 25 minutes

Cook's Note

Chilli Chicken: For a much hotter version, prepare as above but add 2–10 chopped green chillies instead of the peppers – the quantity of chillies depends on your heat threshold!

6 tablespoons ghee
1 teaspoon white cumin seeds
1 teaspoon black mustard seeds
2–6 garlic cloves, finely chopped
5 cm/2 inch piece fresh root
    ginger, thinly sliced
1 large onion, thinly sliced
750 g/1½ lb skinless, boneless
    chicken breasts, cubed
1 tablespoon mild curry paste
½ red pepper, cored, deseeded
    and chopped
½ green pepper, cored, deseeded
    and chopped
1 tablespoon chopped fresh
    coriander leaves
1–2 tablespoons water

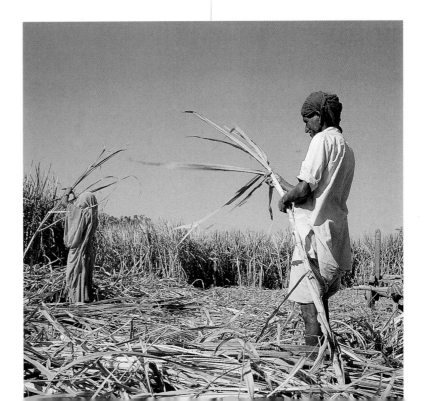

Chicken Makhani

750 g/1½ lb skinless, boneless
    chicken breasts or thighs, cut
    into 5 cm/2 inch pieces
3 tablespoons vegetable oil
MARINADE:
3 large red chillies, deseeded and
    chopped
4 garlic cloves, crushed
2 teaspoons dry-roasted cumin
    seeds, crushed
1 teaspoon garam masala
½ teaspoon salt
2 tablespoons fresh coriander
    leaves
4 tablespoons lemon juice
150 g/5 oz natural yogurt
SAUCE:
1.5 kg/3 lb ripe tomatoes,
    quartered
50 g/2 oz butter
150 ml/¼ pint double cream
salt
TO GARNISH:
sprigs of fresh coriander
red chilli, diced
Naan bread, to serve
    (see page 122)

Tomatoes and butter are the characteristic ingredients of a makhani, a refined and elegant dish.

1 Start by making the marinade. Place the chillies, garlic and cumin seeds in a blender or food processor and blend briefly. Add the remaining marinade ingredients and work to a paste.
2 Transfer the marinade to a non-metallic bowl. Add the chicken pieces to the marinade, turning to coat them evenly. Cover and refrigerate for 3 hours.
3 Meanwhile, prepare the sauce. Place the tomatoes in a large pan and cook them gently, with no added water, for about 20 minutes or until they are tender. Rub them through a fine sieve into a clean pan. Simmer the tomato pulp, stirring occasionally, for 30–40 minutes, until it is thick and reduced.
4 Stir in the butter and some salt and cook the sauce over a medium heat, stirring often, for a further 30 minutes, until it is thick. Stir in the cream and heat it through. Taste and adjust the amount of salt if necessary and set the sauce aside.
5 Heat the oil in a large, heavy-based frying pan. Remove the chicken pieces from their marinade, reserving the marinade, and fry them gently to seal, for about 5 minutes. Add the marinade to the pan, increase the heat and cook, stirring frequently, for a further 12 minutes, or until the chicken is cooked through.
6 Reduce the heat and pour the tomato sauce over the chicken. Simmer gently for a further 5 minutes.
7 Transfer the chicken to a warmed serving dish and garnish with fresh coriander leaves and diced chilli. Serve with Naan bread.

Serves 4
Preparation time: 30 minutes, plus marinating
Cooking time: 2 hours

Kashmiri Chicken

125 g/4 oz butter
3 large onions, finely sliced
10 peppercorns
1 cardamom pod
5 cm/2 inch piece cinnamon stick
5 cm/2 inch piece fresh root
    ginger, chopped
2 garlic cloves, finely chopped
1 teaspoon chilli powder
2 teaspoons paprika
1.5 kg/3 lb chicken pieces, skinned
250 g/8 oz natural yogurt
salt

The addition of natural yogurt towards the end of the cooking time gives this dish a deliciously mild and creamy flavour, which makes a wonderful contrast to all the spices.

1 Melt the butter in a deep, lidded frying pan. Add the onions, peppercorns, cardamom and cinnamon and fry until the onions are golden. Add the ginger, garlic, chilli powder, paprika and salt to taste and fry for 2 minutes, stirring occasionally.
2 Add the chicken pieces and fry until browned. Gradually add the yogurt, stirring constantly. Cover and cook gently for about 30 minutes. Serve hot.

Serves 6
Preparation time: 10 minutes
Cooking time: 40–45 minutes

Chicken Curry

1 Place the garlic, ginger, turmeric, cumin, chilli powder, pepper, fresh coriander, yogurt and salt to taste in a large bowl. Mix well, add the chicken pieces and leave for 4 hours, turning occasionally.
2 Heat the oil in a pan, add the onions and fry until golden. Add the chicken and the marinade. Bring to simmering point, cover and cook for about 30 minutes, until the chicken is tender.

Serves 4
Preparation time: 5–10 minutes, plus marinating
Cooking time: 40 minutes

2 garlic cloves, chopped
5 cm/2 inch piece fresh root
  ginger, chopped
1 teaspoon turmeric
2 teaspoons cumin seeds, ground
1 teaspoon chilli powder
1 teaspoon pepper
3 tablespoons finely chopped
  fresh coriander
500 g/1 lb natural yogurt
1 kg/2 lb chicken pieces, skinned
4 tablespoons vegetable oil
2 onions, chopped
salt

'Eating while seated makes one of large size; eating while standing makes one strong.'

Proverb

Chicken with Spinach

3 tablespoons vegetable oil
2 onions, chopped
2 garlic cloves, crushed
2.5 cm/1 inch piece fresh root
   ginger, chopped
2 teaspoons ground coriander
1 teaspoon chilli powder
750 g/1½ lb chicken legs and thighs,
   skinned
750 g/1½ lb spinach
2–3 tablespoons milk, to mix
   (optional)
salt

1 Heat the oil in a large frying pan. Add the onions and fry until soft and golden. Add the garlic, ginger, ground coriander, chilli powder and season with salt to taste, then fry gently for 2 minutes, stirring constantly.

2 Add the chicken pieces and fry on all sides until browned. Add the spinach, stir well, cover and simmer for 35 minutes, until the chicken is tender.

3 If the mixture becomes too dry during cooking, stir in a little milk. If there is too much liquid left at the end of cooking, uncover the pan and cook for a few minutes more until the liquid has evaporated.

Serves 4
Preparation time: 10 minutes
Cooking time: 45–50 minutes

Chicken and Dhal Curry

250 g/8 oz red lentils
  (masoor dhal)
600 ml/1 pint water
3 tablespoons vegetable oil
2 onions, finely chopped
2 garlic cloves, crushed
2.5 cm/1 inch piece fresh root
  ginger, finely chopped
1 tablespoon ground coriander
1 teaspoon ground cumin
½ teaspoon turmeric
½ teaspoon ground cloves
2 teaspoons chilli powder
750 g/1½ lb chicken thighs
salt

1 Wash the lentils in several changes of cold water, then leave to soak in a bowl of clean water for 1 hour. Drain the lentils and boil in the measured water with 1 teaspoon salt added, for about 1 hour, until soft. Drain and set aside.

2 Heat the oil in a pan, add the onions, garlic and ginger and fry for about 5 minutes. Add the spices and salt to taste and fry gently for 10 minutes. If the mixture becomes too dry, add 2 tablespoons water. Add the chicken thighs and fry until golden all over. Add the cooked lentils, cover and simmer for about 30 minutes, or until the chicken is tender.

Serves 4
Preparation time: 10–15 minutes, plus standing
Cooking time: 1¾–2 hours

Cook's Note
Dhal are pulses or lentils and are widely used in Indian cooking. There are many different types and all are good sources of protein. Masoor dhal are widely available and are split, skinless lentils, known as red lentils, although they are actually pinky orange in colour. Recipes vary but, on the whole, lentils do not really need soaking before use. They should, however, be washed in several changes of cold water before being cooked.

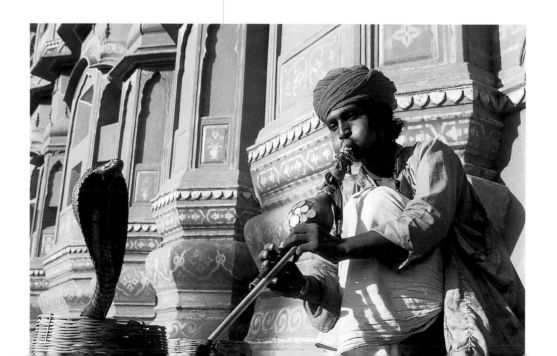

Tandoori Chicken

1 Mix together the chilli powder, pepper, salt and lemon juice. Slash the chicken all over and rub the mixture into the cuts. Set aside for 1 hour.

2 Place the yogurt, garlic, ginger, chillies and coriander and cumin seeds in a blender or food processor and work to a paste. Spread it all over the chicken. Cover and leave in the refrigerator overnight. The next day return the chicken to room temperature before cooking.

3 Place the chicken on a rack in a roasting tin and pour over half the melted butter. Cook in a preheated oven, 200°C/400°F/Gas Mark 6, for 1–1¼ hours, or until tender. Baste occasionally and pour over the remaining butter halfway through the cooking time.

Serves 4

Preparation time: 10 minutes, plus marinating
Cooking time: 1–1¼ hour
Oven temperature: 200°C/400°F/Gas Mark 6

Cook's Notes

If preferred, the chicken can be spit-roasted for about 1 hour, using all the butter at the start. The typical red colour of tandoori chicken comes from a food colouring which is obtainable from Asian food shops. It has been omitted from this recipe because many people are allergic to it.

½–1 teaspoon chilli powder
1 teaspoon pepper
1 teaspoon salt
2 tablespoons lemon juice
1.5 kg/3 lb oven-ready chicken, skinned
4 tablespoons natural yogurt
3 garlic cloves
5 cm/2 inch piece fresh root ginger
2 small dried red chillies
1 tablespoon coriander seeds
2 teaspoons cumin seeds
50 g/2 oz butter, melted

Chicken Stuffed with Rice

125 g/4 oz basmati rice
2 onions, roughly chopped
2 garlic cloves, roughly chopped
5 cm/2 inch piece fresh root ginger
1 teaspoon poppy seeds
8 peppercorns
300 g/10 oz natural yogurt
1 teaspoon garam masala
1.5 kg/3 lb oven-ready chicken
3 tablespoons ghee
½ teaspoon chilli powder
50 g/2 oz sultanas
50 g/2 oz slivered almonds
450 ml/¾ pint water
salt
sprigs of fresh coriander, to garnish

A chicken is stuffed with flavoured basmati rice and cooked in the oven.

1 Place the rice in a bowl of cold water and leave to soak for 1 hour.
2 Place the onions, garlic, ginger, poppy seeds, peppercorns and half the yogurt in a blender or food processor and work to a paste. Stir in the garam masala and add salt to taste.
3 Prick the chicken all over with a fork and rub in the blended mixture. Leave to stand for 1 hour. Drain the rice.
4 Heat 1 tablespoon of the ghee in a pan, add the rice and fry for 3 minutes, stirring constantly. Add the chilli powder, sultanas, almonds and salt to taste and stir well. Pour in the water and simmer for about 10 minutes, until the rice is almost tender and the water is absorbed. Leave to cool.
5 When the rice is cold, use it to stuff the chicken; sew up both ends. Place on a baking tray and cook in a preheated oven, 190°C/375°F/Gas Mark 5 for 1 hour 20 minutes, or until the juices run clear. If the chicken appears to be browning too quickly, lay a piece of kitchen foil over the top.
6 Remove the chicken and allow to rest. Add the remaining yogurt to the juices in the tray and some water, if necessary, a spoonful at a time, stirring until it is all absorbed. Add more salt if necessary. Serve the chicken in joints or thick slices with the sauce, garnished with fresh coriander sprigs.

Serves 4
Preparation time: 15 minutes, plus soaking and marinating
Cooking time: 1 hour 15 minutes
Oven temperature: 190°C/375°F/Gas Mark 5

Chicken Bhuna

3 tablespoons ghee
8 dried curry leaves
1 teaspoon black mustard seeds
1 large onion, chopped
4 garlic cloves, chopped
2.5 cm/1 inch piece fresh root
   ginger, chopped
1 tablespoon curry powder
1 teaspoon garam masala
1 teaspoon ground cumin
1 teaspoon ground coriander
2 teaspoons chilli powder
750 g/1½ lb skinless, boneless
   chicken breasts or thighs, cut
   into 2.5 cm/1 inch cubes
1 teaspoon salt
150 ml/¼ pint water

Serve this dry chicken curry with Indian flat breads, such as Chapati or Paratha (see pages 124 and 125).

1 Heat the ghee in a heavy-based frying pan, crumble the curry leaves and add them to the pan with the mustard seeds. Fry them over a gentle heat for 1 minute.
2 Place the onion, garlic and ginger in a blender or food processor and blend to a coarse paste. Add this paste to the fried curry leaves and mustard seeds and cook gently for a further 5 minutes.
3 Add the curry powder, garam masala, cumin, ground coriander and chilli powder to the pan, and cook, stirring, for 2 minutes.
4 Add the chicken, salt and water. Stir to coat the chicken evenly in the spice mixture, then cover the pan and cook over a gentle heat, stirring occasionally, for 20 minutes, or until the chicken is tender.
5 Remove the lid, increase the heat and cook the curry for a further 3–5 minutes, until thick and dry. Taste and adjust the seasoning if necessary and serve the curry immediately.

Serves 4–6
Preparation time: 10 minutes
Cooking time: 30–35 minutes

Butter Chicken

1 Combine the marinade ingredients in a blender or food processor, and set aside for the flavours to infuse.

2 Put the chicken pieces into a bowl, add the vinegar, mixing well, and set aside for 1–2 hours. Spoon the marinade into the bowl containing the chicken and vinegar and mix well. Cover and refrigerate overnight or for up to 24 hours.

3 Transfer the chicken pieces and all the marinade to a roasting tin. Place in a preheated oven, 160°C/325°F/Gas Mark 3, and bake for 20 minutes.

4 Meanwhile, make the sauce. Heat the ghee in a large frying pan or wok and stir-fry the cumin seeds for 1 minute. Add the onion and stir-fry until it is crisp and golden. Add the cream and garam masala and simmer gently.

5 As soon as the chicken is cooked, transfer it to the sauce in the frying pan or wok and mix well. Transfer to a warmed serving dish and serve immediately, sprinkled with chopped mixed herbs.

Serves 4

Preparation time: 10 minutes, plus marinating
Cooking time: 20 minutes
Oven temperature: 160°C/325°F/Gas Mark 3

750 g/1½ lb skinless, boneless
  chicken breasts, cubed
7 tablespoons vinegar
1 tablespoon chopped mixed
  herbs, to garnish
MARINADE:
2–6 garlic cloves
5 cm/2 inch piece fresh root ginger
2 tablespoons mild curry paste
1 tablespoon chopped fresh
  coriander
1–4 green chillies (optional)
1 teaspoon dried mint
150 ml/5 oz natural yogurt
½ teaspoon salt
SAUCE:
6 tablespoons ghee
1 teaspoon white cumin seeds
1 teaspoon black cumin seeds
1 small onion, thinly sliced
7 tablespoons single cream
1 tablespoon garam masala

'Austerity is an ornament, humility is honourable.'

Proverb

Bangalore Chicken Curry

3 tablespoons ghee or vegetable oil
2 onions, thinly sliced
6 garlic cloves, chopped
1 teaspoon turmeric
1½ teaspoons ground dhana jeera
    (¾ teaspoon ground coriander
    and ¾ teaspoon ground cumin)
40 g/1½ oz fresh coriander leaves
3 large green chillies, deseeded and
    chopped
1.75 g/3½ lb chicken, jointed into
    8 pieces
150 ml/¼ pint chicken stock
300 ml/½ pint coconut milk
1 tablespoon lemon juice
salt
TO GARNISH:
sprigs of fresh coriander
yellow chilli, diced
boiled rice, to serve (optional)

This 'green' curry from central southern India is made with a large quantity of fresh coriander and fresh green chillies.

1 Heat the ghee or oil in a large, heavy-based frying pan. Add the onions and fry over a medium heat, stirring frequently, for about 5 minutes, or until they are softened and golden.
2 Stir in the garlic, turmeric and dhana jeera and cook, stirring, for a further 3 minutes.
3 Place the fresh coriander and green chillies in a blender or food processor and blend to a paste. Add this paste to the pan, reduce the heat to low and cook, stirring constantly, for a further 10 minutes.
4 Add the chicken pieces to the pan, turning them in the spice mixture to coat them evenly, then add the stock, coconut milk and a little salt. Bring to the boil, then reduce the heat, cover and simmer, stirring and turning the chicken occasionally, for about 50 minutes, or until the juices run clear. Stir in the lemon juice; taste and adjust the amount of salt if necessary.
5 Transfer the cooked chicken pieces to a warmed serving dish and keep them warm. Increase the heat and boil the curry sauce for 5–8 minutes to thicken it. Pour it over the chicken and serve immediately, with boiled rice, if liked and garnished with coriander and diced chilli.

Serves 4
Preparation time: 20 minutes
Cooking time: 1 hour 20 minutes

Balti Chicken

6 tablespoons vegetable oil
1 onion, chopped
½ teaspoon turmeric
1 teaspoon ground coriander
1 teaspoon ground cumin
1 teaspoon chilli powder
2 tablespoons water
750 g/1½ lb skinless, boneless
    chicken, cubed
1 kg/2 lb tomatoes, chopped
1 large green pepper, cored,
    deseeded and cut into squares
4–6 garlic cloves, chopped
2 fresh green chillies, chopped
salt
Chapatis or Parathas, to serve
    (see pages 124–125)

1 Heat the oil in a large heavy-based frying pan or wok, add the onion and fry until soft. Mix the turmeric, ground coriander, cumin and chilli powder in a small bowl with the water. Stir this spice mixture into the onion and cook until the liquid has dried up – about 3–4 minutes. Add the pieces of chicken and fry on all sides, then add the tomatoes and a pinch of salt to taste. Cover and cook for 15 minutes.

2 Add the green pepper, garlic and chillies. Cook, uncovered, until all the tomato juices have evaporated and the chicken is cooked through. Serve hot with parathas or chapatis.

Serves 4–6
Preparation time: 20 minutes
Cooking time: 30–35 minutes

'When an elephant is in trouble even a frog will kick him.'

Proverb

Chicken & Yogurt Curry with Mint

1 onion, chopped
4 garlic cloves, crushed
15 g/½ oz fresh mint leaves
1 tablespoon grated fresh root
   ginger
3 tablespoons ghee
½ teaspoon saffron threads, infused
   in 2 tablespoons boiling water
   for 10 minutes
2 teaspoons garam masala
1 teaspoon chilli powder
750 g/1½ lb skinless, boneless
   chicken breasts
½ teaspoon salt
100 g/3½ oz natural yogurt
175 g/6 oz tomatoes, chopped
sprigs of mint, to garnish
steamed or boiled rice, to serve
   (optional)

1 Place the onion, garlic, mint leaves and ginger in a blender or food processor and blend to a smooth paste.

2 Heat the ghee in a large, heavy-based pan, add the blended paste and fry gently for 5 minutes.

3 Add the saffron with its infused water, the garam masala and chilli powder and fry for a further 1 minute.

4 Cut each chicken breast into 3 pieces and add the pieces to the pan with the salt. Stir to coat the chicken in the spice mixture and cook for a further 5 minutes, to seal the chicken.

5 Add the yogurt and tomatoes, stir well, cover the pan and simmer gently for 15 minutes, until the chicken is cooked.

6 Remove the lid and simmer uncovered for 45 minutes more to thicken the sauce slightly. Taste the sauce and adjust the amount of salt, if necessary.

7 Transfer the curry to a warmed serving dish, garnish with mint sprigs and serve with steamed or boiled rice, if liked.

Serves 4–6
Preparation time: 15–20 minutes
Cooking time: 1 hour 10 minutes

Special Spiced Balti Chicken

1 Dry-fry the peppercorns, nigella and fennel seeds in a pan over a low heat for 3 minutes, until fragrant. Remove from the pan and grind to a powder, using an electric spice mill or a pestle and mortar.
2 Heat the oil in the pan, add the onion, ginger and garlic and fry, stirring, for 5 minutes, until soft. Add the ground spices, the garam masala, ground coriander, cumin, chilli powder and turmeric. Stir-fry for 3 minutes, then add the water, the coconut milk powder, lemon juice and ½ teaspoon salt. Bring to the boil, stirring, then add the cardamom pods, cinnamon and bay leaf. Simmer, stirring occasionally, for 15–20 minutes, until a glaze forms on top of the liquid.
4 Add the pieces of chicken, the tomatoes and sugar and stir. Cover and cook for 20 minutes, or until the chicken is cooked. Remove and discard the cinnamon stick and bay leaf and serve the balti hot.

Serves 4–6
Preparation time: 20 minutes
Cooking time: 50–60 minutes

½ teaspoon black peppercorns
½ teaspoon nigella seeds (kalonji)
½ teaspoon fennel seeds
2 tablespoons vegetable oil
I onion, chopped
2.5 cm/I inch piece fresh root
   ginger, crushed
I garlic clove, crushed
I tablespoon garam masala
I teaspoon ground coriander
I teaspoon ground cumin
I teaspoon chilli powder
I teaspoon turmeric
450 ml/¾ pint water
50 g/2 oz coconut milk powder
I tablespoon lemon juice
6 cardamom pods, bruised
5 cm/2 inch piece cinnamon stick
I bay leaf
I kg/2 lb skinless, boneless chicken
   thighs, cut into bite-sized pieces
4 ripe tomatoes, skinned,
   deseeded and roughly chopped
¼ teaspoon sugar
salt

fish
& seafood

Fishing is practised along the entire length of India's coastline and on virtually all of its many rivers. Few fishing craft are mechanized, so total catches are low and the annual per capita fish consumption is modest. Kerala in the south is the leading fishing state. The types of fish available in Indian rivers, lakes and seas are different from those found in the colder European waters. Many of the recipes in this section have therefore been adapted for fish, such as cod and haddock, not found in India but commonly available elsewhere.

Kerala Prawn Curry

2 tablespoons groundnut oil
1 onion, finely chopped
3 garlic cloves, crushed
2.5 cm/1 inch piece fresh root
   ginger, peeled and cut into fine
   strips
125 g/4 oz tomatoes, roughly
   chopped
200 ml/7 fl oz coconut milk
½ teaspoon salt
juice of 1 lime
2 teaspoons caster sugar
20 large raw prawns, about
   375 g/12 oz total weight
1 spring onion, sliced into fine
   strips and fried, to garnish
SPICE MIXTURE:
3 tablespoons desiccated coconut,
   lightly toasted
6 small dried red chillies, roughly
   chopped
10 black peppercorns
1 teaspoon cumin seeds
1 teaspoon turmeric

Southern Indian curries like this one are traditionally fairly spicy – the spiciness coming from the number of dried chillies used in the recipe.

1 Grind the ingredients for the spice mixture to a fine powder, using an electric spice mill or a pestle and mortar.
2 Heat the groundnut oil in a large heavy-based pan, add the onion, garlic and ginger, and cook, stirring occasionally, for about 3 minutes, until softened.
3 Stir in the ground spice mixture and cook, stirring constantly, for a further 2 minutes.
4 Add the tomatoes, coconut milk and season with salt, then simmer for 6–8 minutes to reduce the sauce and thicken it slightly.
5 Stir in the lime juice and sugar, then add the prawns and simmer the curry gently for about 8 minutes, or until the prawns have turned pink.
6 Transfer the curry to a warmed serving dish and scatter over the spring onion. Serve immediately.

Serves 4
Preparation time: 10–15 minutes
Cooking time: 20–25 minutes

Fish Molee

4 x 150 g/5 oz cod or haddock
   fillets
½ teaspoon turmeric
1 teaspoon salt
2 tablespoons ghee or vegetable oil
1 onion, finely chopped
3 garlic cloves, crushed
1 tablespoon freshly grated root
   ginger
1 tablespoon curry powder
2 fresh red chillies, quartered
   lengthways and deseeded
450 ml/¾ pint thick coconut milk

This mild curry, cooked in rich coconut milk, comes from southern India. A similar curry is made in Sri Lanka, where it is called 'white curry'.

1 Rub the fish fillets with the turmeric and salt and set them aside while you prepare the curry sauce.
2 Heat the ghee or oil in a heavy-based pan. Add the onion, garlic and ginger and fry over a gentle heat for about 3 minutes, until softened.
3 Stir in the curry powder and chillies and cook, stirring constantly, for a further 2 minutes.
4 Add the coconut milk and bring to the boil, stirring constantly, then reduce the heat and simmer the sauce for about 5 minutes, or until it has thickened slightly.
5 Add the fish and cook gently for a further 6–8 minutes, or until the fish flakes when tested with the point of a knife. Taste and adjust the seasoning if necessary. Serve hot.

Serves 4
Preparation time: 10 minutes
Cooking time: 20 minutes

Prawn Vindaloo

1 Mix together the dried chillies, malt vinegar, garlic, ginger, mustard seeds and peppercorns in a bowl, then stir in the ground coriander, cumin and turmeric.

2 Heat the vegetable oil in a heavy-based saucepan, stir in the spice mixture and cook over a gentle heat, stirring constantly, for 5 minutes. Add the water to the pan, stir well, then cover and simmer the sauce gently for 15 minutes.

3 Remove the lid from the pan, increase the heat and cook the sauce over a moderate heat for 5 minutes to reduce it to a thick, coating consistency.

4 Stir the salt, sugar and prawns into the sauce. Cook for 3 minutes, or until the prawns are heated through. Serve immediately.

Serves 4
Preparation time: 10 minutes
Cooking time: 30 minutes

6 dried red chillies, deseeded and chopped
150 ml/¼ pint distilled malt vinegar
6 garlic cloves, chopped
2.5 cm/1 inch piece fresh root ginger, grated
1 teaspoon mustard seeds, lightly crushed
20 black peppercorns, lightly crushed
1 tablespoon ground coriander
1 tablespoon ground cumin
1 teaspoon turmeric
2 tablespoons vegetable oil
300 ml/½ pint water
1 teaspoon salt
1 tablespoon soft brown sugar
500 g/1 lb cooked peeled prawns

Steamed Tuna Curry in Banana Leaves

4 x 150 g/5 oz fresh tuna steaks
juice of 1 lime
4 large pieces banana leaf
GREEN CURRY PASTE:
1 tablespoon cumin seeds
2 tablespoons coriander seeds
3 large green chillies, deseeded and
    chopped
25 g/1 oz fresh mint leaves
5 cm/2 inch piece fresh root
    ginger, grated
4 garlic cloves, crushed
25 g/1 oz caster sugar
½ teaspoon salt
75 g/3 oz desiccated coconut
50 ml/2 fl oz malt vinegar
TO GARNISH:
lime wedges
fine strips of lemon rind
1 red chilli, cut into rings

This is a very fresh-tasting curry. If banana leaves are unavailable, wrap the tuna steaks in a double thickness of buttered greaseproof paper for steaming.

1 Place the tuna steaks in a shallow, non-metallic dish and pour over the lime juice. Cover and set aside to marinate while preparing the curry paste.
2 Place the cumin and coriander seeds in a blender or food processor and process briefly. Add the chillies, mint, ginger and garlic, and work for 1 minute to produce a paste. Add the sugar, salt, coconut and vinegar, and blend again until all the ingredients are thoroughly combined.
3 Lay the pieces of banana leaf (or buttered greaseproof paper) on a flat surface. Remove the tuna from the lime juice and place a steak in the centre of each banana leaf. Spread the green curry paste over the tuna, completely covering the fish. Wrap up the banana leaves to enclose the fish, and secure with cocktail sticks.
4 Steam the fish over a pan of boiling water for 18–20 minutes, or until the fish flakes when tested with the point of a knife.
5 Garnish the steamed fish with lime wedges and chilli rings.

Serves 4
Preparation time: 15 minutes
Cooking time: 20 minutes

Cook's Note
There are dozens of varieties of chilli peppers. These range from mildly warm to blisteringly hot and can vary in length from 5 mm (¼ inch) to 30 cm (12 inches). Fresh chillies should look bright and shiny, with no markings on the skin. To prepare chillies, pull off their stalks and cut them in half lengthways. Doing this under cold running water will prevent irritating fumes from rising into your face. Whether or not you remove the seeds depends on your personal preference.

Madras Fish Curry

750 g/1½ lb skinless cod fillet, cut
   into 10 cm/4 inch pieces
1 teaspoon turmeric
½ teaspoon salt
1 tablespoon dried tamarind
300 ml/½ pint boiling water
4 tablespoons groundnut oil
8 curry leaves
2 teaspoons nigella seeds (kalonji)
2 onions, thinly sliced
2 large green chillies, deseeded and
   thinly sliced
2 tablespoons Madras curry paste
4 small tomatoes, quartered
4 tablespoons chopped fresh
   coriander
TO SERVE: (OPTIONAL)
steamed rice
Naan bread (see page 122)

A hot curry with the added tartness of tamarind – a favourite ingredient in Indian fish curries.

1 Rub the cod fillet pieces with the turmeric and salt, and place in a shallow, non-metallic dish.

2 Soak the tamarind in the boiling water for 10 minutes, then strain the pulp through a sieve set over a bowl, pressing it against the sieve to extract as much flavour from the pulp as possible. Discard the pulp and pour the tamarind liquid over the fish. Cover and marinate for 1 hour in the refrigerator.

3 Meanwhile, prepare the curry sauce. Heat the groundnut oil in a heavy-based frying pan, add the curry leaves and nigella seeds and cook gently for 1 minute.

4 Stir in the sliced onions and chillies, then cook for a further 3 minutes, until softened but not browned. Stir in the curry paste and cook for a further 2 minutes.

5 Remove the fish from the tamarind liquid and set aside. Add the tamarind liquid to the pan of fried ingredients, with the tomatoes. Stir gently to mix, then simmer the sauce gently for 10 minutes.

6 Add the fish and fresh coriander to the pan, cover and cook for a further 8 minutes, or until the fish is just cooked through. Taste and adjust the seasoning if necessary and serve the curry hot, with steamed rice or Naan bread, if liked.

Serves 4
Preparation time: 25 minutes, plus marinating
Cooking time: 25 minutes

Cook's Note
The tamarind tree grows extensively throughout India. Its long fruit pods contain seeds surrounded by a sticky pulp, which produces the acidic flavouring widely used in Indian cooking. Tamarind is most usually available in the form of a rectangular block of compressed pulp and seeds, which requires soaking in hot water to extract the sour juice.

Balti Prawns

1 Melt the ghee in a large heavy-based frying pan or wok, add the onion and ginger and fry gently for 4–5 minutes, or until the onion is soft, then add the garlic.

2 Meanwhile, in a small bowl mix the ground coriander, ginger, turmeric, cumin and chilli powder to a paste with the vinegar, then add this paste to the pan and stir-fry for a further 3 minutes.

3 Add the cooked prawns with the pieces of pepper and turn gently with a wooden spoon until they are well coated with the spices. Add the water and the tomato purée and stir well. Bring to the boil, simmer for 1–2 minutes, then serve immediately, garnished with fresh coriander.

Serves 4
Preparation time: 10 minutes
Cooking time: 10–15 minutes

50 g/2 oz ghee
I small onion, sliced
2.5 cm/I inch piece fresh root
    ginger, chopped
2 garlic cloves, sliced
2 teaspoons ground coriander
½ teaspoon ground ginger
I teaspoon turmeric
½ teaspoon ground cumin
½ teaspoon chilli powder
2 tablespoons vinegar
500 g/I lb cooked peeled prawns
I red or green pepper, cored,
    deseeded and cut into squares
200 ml/7 fl oz water
I tablespoon tomato purée
chopped fresh coriander leaves, to
    garnish

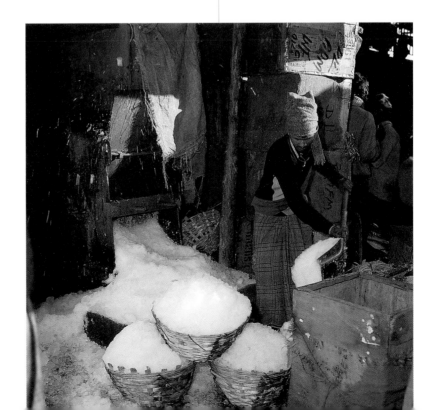

Balti Seafood Curry

1–2 tablespoons vegetable oil
2 onions, finely chopped
2 garlic cloves, crushed
1 green pepper, cored, deseeded
   and sliced
2 tablespoons curry powder
2 teaspoons chilli powder
25 g/1 oz plain flour
600 ml/1 pint hot water
500 g/1 lb white fish fillets, skinned
   and cubed
125 g/4 oz cooked shelled mussels
125 g/4 oz cooked peeled prawns
4 tomatoes, skinned, quartered
   and deseeded
salt and pepper
red chillies, cut into thin strips,
   to garnish
steamed or boiled rice, to serve
   (optional)

This is quite a hot curry, as it contains curry powder and chilli powder.

1 Heat the oil in a large, heavy-based frying pan or wok, add the onions, garlic and green pepper and fry until soft but not brown. Add the curry powder, chilli powder and flour and cook gently for about 2–3 minutes.
2 Gradually add the hot water, stirring constantly. Bring the mixture to the boil, lower the heat to a gentle simmer, then add the pieces of white fish and cook for 15 minutes.
3 Add the cooked mussels and prawns and the tomatoes to the pan, season with salt and pepper to taste and simmer for a further 5 minutes.
4 Garnish with strips of chilli and serve immediately with rice, if liked.

Serves 4–6
Preparation time: 20 minutes
Cooking time: 30 minutes

'He who rides a tiger is afraid to dismount.'

Proverb

Hot & Sour Prawns

125 g/4 oz dried tamarind
300 ml/½ pint hot water
2 teaspoons sugar (optional)
2 green chillies
25 g/1 oz fresh coriander leaves
2 garlic cloves
1 onion, roughly chopped
2 tablespoons vegetable oil
1 teaspoon fennel seeds
1 teaspoon chilli powder
1 teaspoon salt
500 g/1 lb large raw peeled prawns

1 Soak the tamarind in the hot water for 30 minutes, then strain the pulp through a sieve set over a bowl, pressing it against the sieve to extract as much flavour from the pulp as possible. Discard the pulp and stir the sugar into the tamarind water if you do not like a sour curry. Set aside.
2 Put the chillies, fresh coriander, garlic and onion in a blender or food processor and work to a paste.
3 Heat the oil in a pan. Add the fennel seeds and fry for 30 seconds. Add the prepared spice paste, chilli powder and salt and fry gently for 5 minutes, stirring occasionally. Add the tamarind water, stir well, bring to the boil, then simmer for 5 minutes.
4 Add the prawns, cover and simmer for 10 minutes, or until cooked through and pink in colour, stirring occasionally. Serve hot.

Serves 4
Preparation time: 15 minutes, plus soaking
Cooking time: 25 minutes

Vinegar Fish

1 teaspoon turmeric
1 teaspoon salt
500 g/1 lb haddock or cod steaks
3 tablespoons vegetable oil
2 onions, sliced
2–3 green chillies, thinly sliced
2 garlic cloves, crushed
2.5 cm/1 inch piece fresh root
    ginger, cut into fine strips
2 tablespoons white wine vinegar
4 tablespoons water
sprigs of fresh coriander, to garnish

1 Mix the turmeric and salt together on a plate. Coat the fish in the mixture, adding more turmeric and salt, if necessary.
2 Heat the oil in a large frying pan, add the fish and fry gently on both sides for 1–2 minutes. Lift out the fish and set aside on a plate.
3 Add the onions, chillies, garlic and ginger to the pan and fry, stirring, until golden. Stir in the vinegar and water. Return the fish to the pan, cover and cook gently for 5–6 minutes, or until it is cooked through.
4 Transfer the fish to a warmed serving dish and serve, garnished with coriander sprigs.

Serves 4
Preparation time: 10 minutes
Cooking time: 15 minutes

Fish with Yogurt

Cod steaks are marinated in yogurt, then cooked in a fragrant paste.

1 Place the fish in a shallow, non-metallic dish and sprinkle with the salt. Add the yogurt and leave the fish to marinate for about 1 hour, turning once or twice.

2 Heat 1 tablespoon of the oil in a pan, add 1 of the onions and fry until crisp. Place this, together with the remaining onion, the ginger, green chillies and garlic, in a blender or food processor and work to a smooth paste.

3 Heat the remaining oil in a large frying pan with a lid. Fry the fenugreek seeds for 30 seconds, then add the prepared paste and fry until it starts to brown. Now add the fish and yogurt. Stir carefully and spoon the mixture over the fish. Cover the pan and simmer for 5–10 minutes, or until cooked through; if drying too fast, add 2 tablespoons of water; if too liquid, uncover and allow to dry out.

4 Transfer to a warmed serving dish and garnish with coriander sprigs, if liked.

Serves 4
Preparation time: 10 minutes, plus marinating
Cooking time: 15 minutes

1 kg/2 lb cod steaks
1 teaspoon salt
150 g/5 oz natural yogurt
4 tablespoons vegetable oil
2 onions, finely sliced
2.5 cm/1 inch piece fresh root
    ginger, thinly sliced
4 green chillies
2 garlic cloves
1 teaspoon fenugreek seeds
sprigs of fresh coriander, to garnish
    (optional)

Coconut Fish

2 tablespoons vegetable oil
4 green chillies, deseeded and
    chopped
2 garlic cloves, finely chopped
2.5 cm/1 inch piece fresh root
    ginger, finely chopped
125 g/4 oz creamed coconut
1 kg/2 lb thick haddock fillets,
    skinned and cubed
8 tablespoons lemon juice
salt
TO GARNISH:
coconut shavings
fine strips of lemon rind

This simple fish curry is light and fresh, with the combination of ginger, coconut and lemon juice resulting in an aromatic dish, full of flavour. It is also quick and simple to prepare.

1 Heat the oil in a large frying pan, add the chillies, garlic and ginger and fry gently for 3 minutes. Add the creamed coconut and, when bubbling, add the pieces of fish and season with salt to taste. Stir well.
2 Cook for 3–4 minutes, stirring constantly and breaking up the fish as it cooks.
3 As soon as all the fish is cooked through, pour in the lemon juice, stir well and serve, garnished with coconut shavings and strips of lemon rind.

Serves 4
Preparation time: 10–15 minutes
Cooking time: 10 minutes

'Follow the river and you'll get to the sea.'

Proverb

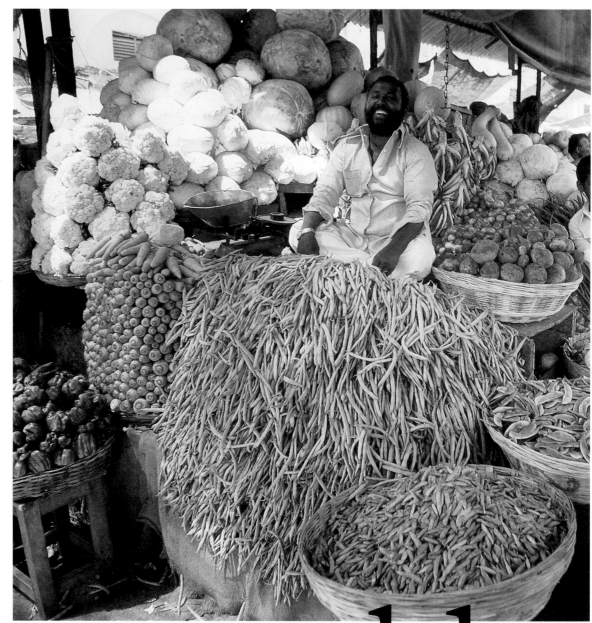

vegetables

Since many Indians are vegetarian, over the years Indian cooks have created a great variety of ways of cooking everyday vegetables. Pulses – dried beans, split peas and lentils – are a staple in India and help provide a large measure of the daily protein for families who eat meat only rarely or not at all. Some pulses can be hard to digest and are almost always cooked with seasonings that make the beans more digestible, such as ginger, asafoetida or turmeric.

Cauliflower Pachadi

375 g/12 oz cauliflower florets
150 ml/¼ pint buttermilk
1 teaspoon salt
3 tablespoons ghee
1 large onion, thinly sliced
2 garlic cloves, crushed
1 tablespoon freshly grated root
   ginger
1 teaspoon mustard seeds
1 teaspoon black mustard seeds
1 teaspoon turmeric
25 g/1 oz desiccated coconut
150 ml/¼ pint water
2 tablespoons chopped fresh
   coriander
pepper
whole green chillies, to garnish

This is a traditional dish from Kerala in southern India, in which cauliflower is marinated in buttermilk before cooking.

1 Place the cauliflower florets in a bowl with the buttermilk, salt and some pepper. Mix well to combine the ingredients and set aside for 2 hours to allow the cauliflower to marinate.

2 Heat the ghee in a heavy-based pan, add the onion, garlic and ginger and fry over a gentle heat, stirring occasionally, for about 8 minutes, until softened and lightly golden.

3 Add the mustard seeds, turmeric and coconut and cook for a further 3 minutes, stirring constantly.

4 Stir in the cauliflower with its buttermilk marinade and the water. Bring the curry to the boil, then reduce the heat, cover the pan and simmer gently for 12 minutes, or until the cauliflower is tender.

5 Remove the lid, adjust the seasoning to taste, if necessary, and stir in the chopped fresh coriander. Increase the heat and cook for a further 3–4 minutes to thicken the sauce. Garnish with whole chillies and serve hot as a vegetable accompaniment to other curries, or with steamed rice or Indian bread such as Naan (see page 122).

Serves 4
Preparation time: 10 minutes, plus marinating
Cooking time: 30 minutes

Mushroom Curry *pictured*

2 tablespoons ghee or vegetable oil
3 garlic cloves, crushed
1 teaspoon freshly grated root
    ginger
6 spring onions, sliced
1 tablespoon curry powder
½ teaspoon mustard seeds
300 g/10 oz button mushrooms,
    halved
300 g/10 oz flat mushrooms,
    thickly sliced
1 teaspoon salt
1 teaspoon garam masala
150 ml/¼ pint thick coconut milk
2 tablespoons lemon juice
sprigs of fresh coriander, to garnish

1 Heat the ghee or oil in a heavy-based frying pan. Add the garlic, ginger and spring onions and fry over a gentle heat, stirring occasionally, for 2 minutes, or until softened.

2 Stir in the curry powder and mustard seeds and cook for a further 1 minute. Add the prepared mushrooms and the salt. Stir well to mix, then cook, covered, for a further 5 minutes, stirring occasionally.

3 Add the garam masala and coconut milk and cook, uncovered, for a further 4–5 minutes, until the sauce has thickened slightly.

4 Stir in the lemon juice. Adjust the seasoning, if necessary, then serve immediately, garnished with coriander sprigs.

Serves 4
Preparation time: 10–15 minutes
Cooking time: 15 minutes

Spinach Paneer

375 g/12 oz young leaf spinach,
    washed and dried
2 tablespoons ghee
250 g/8 oz paneer, cut into
    2.5 cm/1 inch cubes
1 large onion, chopped
2 garlic cloves, crushed
1 large green chilli, deseeded and
    chopped
1 tablespoon grated fresh root
    ginger
1 teaspoon turmeric
1 teaspoon ground coriander
1 teaspoon chilli powder
½ teaspoon ground cumin
½ teaspoon salt

Paneer is Indian curd cheese and is available from good Indian grocers.

1 Steam the spinach over a pan of boiling water for 3–4 minutes, until it has wilted, then leave to cool. Place the spinach in a blender or food processor and work briefly to purée. Set aside.

2 Heat the ghee in a heavy-based pan, add the cubes of paneer and fry, turning occasionally, for 10 minutes, or until they are golden all over. Remove them from the pan and set aside.

3 Add the onion, garlic, chilli and ginger to the hot ghee and fry gently over a low heat, stirring constantly for 5 minutes, until softened. Stir in the turmeric, ground coriander, chilli powder and cumin and fry for a further minute.

4 Add the puréed spinach and salt, stir well to combine, cover the pan and simmer gently for 5 minutes.

5 Stir in the fried paneer and cook, covered, for a further 5 minutes. Adjust the seasoning, if necessary, and serve immediately.

Serves 4
Preparation time: 15 minutes
Cooking time: 30 minutes

Bombay Potatoes

4 tablespoons vegetable oil
½ quantity Curry Purée
 (see page 48)
I tablespoon mild curry paste
2 tomatoes, thinly sliced
750 g/1½ lb cooked new potatoes
Aromatic Salt (see Cook's Note)
I tablespoon chopped mixed
 herbs, to garnish

Small new potatoes are perfect for this medium-hot curry.

1 Heat the oil in a large frying pan or wok and stir-fry the curry purée for 2–3 minutes. Add the curry paste and bring the mixture to simmering point. Add the sliced tomatoes.
2 When the sauce is simmering again, add the potatoes and stir gently until they are heated through. Season with aromatic salt to taste, sprinkle with the chopped mixed herbs and serve immediately.

Serves 4
Preparation time: 5 minutes
Cooking time: 10 minutes

Cook's Note
Spicy aromatic salt is widely used in Indian cooking, sprinkled over a variety of dishes. It is made by mixing dry-fried spices (see page 50) with sea salt and grinding the mixture as finely or as coarsely as you wish, in an electric spice mill or using a pestle and mortar.
Combine 75 g/3 oz sea salt with 1 teaspoon each of dry-fried coriander and cumin seeds, and ½ teaspoon each of dry-fried Szechuan pepper, fennel seeds, allspice and sesame seeds. Store the aromatic salt in a small airtight jar in a cool, dry place, where it will keep indefinitely.

Spinach Bhajee

1 If you are using fresh spinach, wash it in cold water very thoroughly. Chop the leaves coarsely and boil them for 5 minutes in just the water clinging to the leaves. Strain, discarding the water. Frozen spinach should be defrosted and drained.

2 Heat the oil in a large frying pan or wok. Stir-fry the spices for 1 minute, then add the garlic and stir-fry for 1 minute more. Add the onion and stir-fry for 3 more minutes. Blend in the curry paste and bring the mixture to simmering point. Add the spinach and continue to cook, stirring frequently, until the spinach has heated through and the flavours have blended – about 5–7 minutes. Season with salt to taste and serve immediately.

Serves 4
Preparation time: 5–15 minutes
Cooking time: 15 minutes

750 g/1½ lb fresh or frozen spinach
2 tablespoons vegetable oil
1–4 garlic cloves, chopped
1 large onion, chopped
1 tablespoon mild curry paste
salt
SPICES:
1 teaspoon white cumin seeds
1 teaspoon sesame seeds
1 teaspoon black mustard seeds
½ teaspoon nigella seeds (kalonji)
   (optional)

Mixed Vegetable Bhajee

1 Slice the vegetables into bite-sized pieces and blanch them briefly in a large saucepan of boiling water. Drain, refresh in cold water and drain again if you wish to prepare the bhajee at a later stage, or use the blanched vegetables hot straight away.

2 Heat the oil in a large frying pan or wok. Add the cumin, mustard and coriander seeds and stir-fry for 1 minute. Add the curry purée and stir-fry for 5–6 minutes more. Mix in the curry paste and the sliced tomatoes. When the mixture is bubbling, add the prepared vegetables, the chopped fresh coriander and garam masala. Simmer until the vegetables are heated through and are as tender as you like. Season with salt to taste and serve immediately.

Serves 4
Preparation time: 15 minutes
Cooking time: 15–20 minutes

750 g/1½ lb mixed vegetables,
   e.g. large potatoes, carrots,
   cauliflower florets, celery
   sticks, broccoli florets, baby
   sweetcorn cobs
3 tablespoons vegetable oil
1 teaspoon white cumin seeds
1 teaspoon black mustard seeds
¼ teaspoon coriander seeds
1 quantity Curry Purée
   (see page 48)
1 tablespoon mild curry paste
3 tomatoes, thinly sliced
1 tablespoon chopped fresh
   coriander
2 teaspoons garam masala
salt

Yogurt Curry *pictured*

500 g/1 lb natural yogurt
2 tablespoons gram flour (besan)
2 tablespoons vegetable oil
½ teaspoon ground cumin
½ teaspoon ground coriander
2 garlic cloves, crushed
2 green chillies, finely chopped
2 red chillies, finely chopped
1 teaspoon turmeric
salt
1 tablespoon chopped fresh
    coriander leaves
6 curry leaves
TO GARNISH:
curry leaves
1 red chilli, cut into rings

1 Mix the yogurt and gram flour together.
2 Heat the oil in a pan, add the cumin, ground coriander, garlic and chillies and fry for 1 minute. Stir in the turmeric, then immediately pour in the yogurt mixture. Add salt to taste and simmer, uncovered, for 10 minutes, stirring occasionally.
3 Add the chopped fresh coriander and the curry leaves and continue cooking for a further 5 minutes.
4 Transfer to a warmed serving dish and serve, garnished with curry leaves and chilli rings. Remove the curry leaves before eating.

Serves 4
Preparation time: 5 minutes
Cooking time: 20–25 minutes

Hyderabadi Aubergines

vegetable oil or mustard oil, for
    shallow-frying
750 g/1½ lb aubergines, cut
    lengthways into quarters
125 g/4 oz dried tamarind
2 large onions, sliced
1 teaspoon mustard seeds
125 g/4 oz ghee
1½ teaspoons ground coriander
1 fresh green chilli, deseeded and
    chopped
½ teaspoon chilli powder
1 tablespoon desiccated coconut
3 garlic cloves, chopped
1 teaspoon turmeric
1 teaspoon garam masala
1 teaspoon sugar
3 bay leaves

1 Heat a little oil in a frying pan and fry the aubergines until the skins just turn crisp and brown. Remove and drain on kitchen paper.
2 Place the tamarind in a bowl with enough boiling water to cover and leave to soak.
3 Fry the onions and mustard seeds in the ghee in a large pan until brown, then add the ground coriander and green chilli and fry for 5 minutes. Add the chilli powder, coconut, garlic, turmeric and garam masala and fry for 3 minutes further.
4 Strain the tamarind liquid through a sieve set over a bowl, pressing it against the sieve to extract as much flavour from the pulp as possible. Discard the pulp and add the tamarind liquid to the pan, with the sugar. Stir well and add the aubergines. Cover and cook for 10–15 minutes, until the aubergines are tender, stirring occasionally.
5 Fry the bay leaves in a little hot oil for a few seconds and pour over the aubergines just before serving.

Serves 4
Preparation time: 5 minutes
Cooking time: 20–25 minutes

Balti Mixed Vegetables

2–3 tablespoons vegetable oil
1 small onion, chopped
1 garlic clove, crushed
2.5 cm/1 inch piece fresh root
    ginger, grated
1 teaspoon chilli powder
2 teaspoons ground coriander
½ teaspoon turmeric
500 g/1 lb diced mixed vegetables,
    e.g. potatoes, carrots, swede,
    peas, beans, cauliflower
2–3 tomatoes, skinned and
    chopped, or 4 tablespoons
    lemon juice
salt
Naan or Chapatis, to serve
    (see pages 122 and 124)

1 Heat the oil in a large heavy-based frying pan or wok and gently fry the onion for 5–10 minutes, or until lightly browned. Add the garlic, ginger, chilli powder, ground coriander, turmeric and a pinch of salt. Fry for 2–3 minutes, then add the diced vegetables and stir-fry for a further 2–3 minutes.
2 Add either the chopped tomatoes or the lemon juice. Stir well and add a little water. Cover and cook gently for 10–12 minutes, or until the vegetables are tender, adding a little more water if necessary to prevent the vegetables from sticking to the bottom of the pan.
3 Serve immediately with naan or chapatis.

Serves 4
Preparation time: 15 minutes
Cooking time: 20–30 minutes

Balti Pumpkin

1 Soak the tamarind in the hot water for 15 minutes, then strain the pulp through a sieve set over a bowl, pressing it against the sieve to extract as much flavour from the pulp as possible. Discard the pulp and set aside the tamarind liquid.

2 Heat the oil in a large heavy-based frying pan or wok and fry the cumin, mustard, fenugreek and nigella seeds and aniseed for 30 seconds, then add the potatoes and fry for 2–3 minutes. Add the pumpkin, stir well and fry for 4–5 minutes.

3 Stir in the chilli powder, turmeric, ground coriander, sugar and salt to taste and continue frying for 5–6 minutes. Add the tamarind liquid, cover and cook until the potatoes are tender, adding a little more water if necessary to prevent the mixture from sticking to the bottom of the pan. Serve hot.

Serves 4
Preparation time: 25 minutes
Cooking time: 25–30 minutes

20 g/¾ oz dried tamarind
150 ml/¼ pint hot water
3 tablespoons vegetable oil
¼ teaspoon cumin seeds
¼ teaspoon mustard seeds
¼ teaspoon fenugreek seeds
¼ teaspoon nigella seeds (kalonji)
¼ teaspoon aniseed
3 potatoes, cut into chunks
500 g/1 lb pumpkin, cubed
1 teaspoon chilli powder
½ teaspoon turmeric
1 teaspoon ground coriander
1 teaspoon sugar
salt

*'When a man has pity on all living creatures
then only is he noble.'*

Budhha

Bengali Potatoes

750 g/1½ lb small sweet potatoes,
  peeled and chopped
4 tablespoons sunflower or
  mustard blend oil
2 teaspoons panch phoran
  (see Cook's Note)
2–4 garlic cloves, chopped
1 large onion, chopped
1 tablespoon chopped fresh
  coriander
salt

This recipe uses sweet potatoes, which are ideal vegetables for spicy cooking.

1 Cook the sweet potatoes in a large pan of boiling water for about 15 minutes, or until soft.
2 Meanwhile, heat the oil in a large frying pan or wok and stir-fry the panch phoran spices for 1 minute. Add the garlic and stir-fry for 1 minute. Add the onion and stir-fry for 5 minutes more.
3 As soon as the sweet potatoes are cooked, strain them and add to the pan or wok with the chopped fresh coriander. Stir-fry until the ingredients are well blended and heated through. Season with salt to taste and serve immediately.

Serves 4
Preparation time: 10–15 minutes
Cooking time: 20 minutes

Cook's Note
Panch phoran is a Bengali five-spice mixture consisting of equal quantities of whole spices mixed together without dry-roasting or grinding. The mixture is used in one of two ways: it may be fried in oil to impart flavour to the oil before adding the main ingredients, or fried in ghee and stirred into cooked dhal or vegetable dishes just before they are served.
If panch phoran is unavailable, replace the 2 teaspoons of the spice in this recipe with ½ teaspoon white cumin seeds, ½ teaspoon fennel seeds, ½ teaspoon fenugreek seeds, ½ teaspoon black mustard seeds and ½ teaspoon nigella seeds (kalonji).

Dhal

250 g/8 oz red lentils
  (masoor dhal)
300 ml/½ pint water
1 teaspoon garlic powder
1 teaspoon ground cumin
1 teaspoon garam masala
knob of ghee
salt
sprigs of parsley, to garnish

Although red lentils are specified in this recipe, any other types of lentils are suitable for making dhal.

1 Rinse the lentils in several changes of cold water. Place them in a bowl, cover with plenty of water and leave to soak for 30 minutes. Drain well.
2 Bring the measured water to the boil in a large pan. Add the drained soaked lentils. Cook, stirring occasionally until they reach simmering point. Cover the pan and cook for 20 minutes. The lentils should have absorbed the water, but will not yet be cooked.
3 Add the garlic powder, ground cumin and garam masala and simmer the dhal for 10–15 minutes more, stirring occasionally to prevent it sticking. Stir in the ghee and season with salt to taste. Serve immediately, garnished with parsley sprigs.

Serves 4 as an accompaniment
Preparation time: 5 minutes, plus soaking
Cooking time: 35–40 minutes

Dhal with Fried Spices

This recipe involves heating oil or ghee until hot, adding spices and ingredients such as garlic, ginger and onion and sizzling the mixture until very hot. It is then poured directly over food in its serving dish.

1 Rinse the chickpeas and lentils separately in several changes of cold water. Still keeping them separate, soak them in plenty of cold water overnight to allow them to swell and soften.

2 Drain the chickpeas. Bring the measured water to the boil. Add the chickpeas and boil vigorously for 45 minutes. Drain the red lentils and add to the pan. Bring the water back to simmering point, stirring from time to time. Cover the pan and leave to simmer for 20 minutes. Stir the lentils to prevent them sticking to the pan. Add a little water if necessary and continue to simmer.

3 Meanwhile, heat the oil in a large frying pan or wok. Stir-fry the cumin and mustard seeds for 1 minute. Add the garlic and stir-fry for 1 minute. Add the onion and stir-fry for 5 minutes more. Blend in the curry paste. When the mixture is smooth, remove the pan from the heat. Taste the chickpeas and lentils to make sure they are cooked. Drain, if necessary, and transfer to a warmed serving dish. Add the fried mixture to the dhal and season with salt to taste. Serve hot, garnished with parsley sprigs.

Serves 4
Preparation time: 20 minutes, plus soaking
Cooking time: 1¼ hours

50 g/2 oz chickpeas
175 g/6 oz red lentils
   (masoor dhal)
1.2 litres/2 pints water
2 tablespoons vegetable oil
2 teaspoons white cumin seeds
2 teaspoons black mustard seeds
2–4 garlic cloves, finely chopped
1 large onion, thinly sliced
1 tablespoon mild curry paste
salt
sprigs of parsley, to garnish

'Hear twice before you speak once.'

Proverb

rice, chutneys & breads

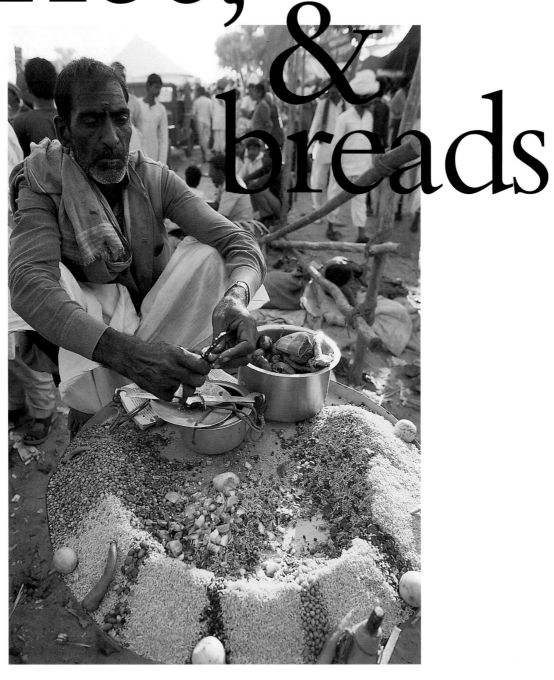

Rice or bread is always served as part of an Indian meal. Basmati rice, grown in the foothills of the Himalayan Mountains, is probably the most popular variety and has a distinctive and aromatic flavour. Most traditional Indian breads are unleavened. To enjoy them at their best they should be made just before the meal and eaten hot. A variety of accompaniments tend to be served with Indian meals, and particularly popular are yogurt relishes, which can be substantial dishes by themselves and provide a cooling contrast to spicy Indian food.

Kitcheri

175 g/6 oz long-grain rice
175 g/6 oz red lentils
    (masoor dhal)
50 g/2 oz butter
1 onion, chopped
1 garlic clove, chopped
5 cm/2 inch piece cinnamon stick
5 cardamom pods
5 cloves
10 peppercorns
450 ml/¾ pint boiling water
salt

A combination of rice and lentils that is cooked with cinnamon, cardamom pods and whole cloves.

1 Wash the rice and lentils separately under running cold water, then leave to soak in fresh cold water for 30 minutes, still keeping them seperate.
2 Melt the butter in a large pan. Add the onion to the pan with the garlic, cinnamon stick, cardamoms, cloves and peppercorns. Fry gently until the onion is soft.
3 Drain the rice and lentils and add the lentils to the pan. Fry gently, stirring, for 2 minutes. Add the water and salt to taste and simmer for about 10 minutes. Add the rice and simmer for 15–20 minutes, until the water is absorbed.
4 Transfer the rice mixture to a warmed serving dish, removing the cinnamon stick before serving.

Serves 4
Preparation time: 10 minutes, plus soaking
Cooking time: 30 minutes

'Rice for good luck.'

Proverb

Coconut Rice

375 g/12 oz basmati rice
450 ml/¾ pint thin coconut milk
½ teaspoon turmeric
8 shallots, roughly chopped
20 peppercorns
1 teaspoon salt
finely chopped spring onions, to
    garnish

1 Wash the basmati rice thoroughly under cold running water, then leave to soak in cold water for 30 minutes; drain.
2 Put the coconut milk in a pan, stir in the turmeric, then add the drained soaked rice. Bring to the boil, then cover and simmer gently for about 10 minutes. Add the shallots, peppercorns and salt and continue cooking gently for another 10 minutes or until the rice is tender. Be careful not to let the rice burn.
3 Transfer to a warmed serving dish and garnish with chopped spring onions.

Serves 4
Preparation time: 35 minutes
Cooking time: 25 minutes

Saffron Rice

375 g/12 oz basmati rice
50 g/2 oz butter or ghee
5 cm/2 inch piece cinnamon stick
6 cardamom pods
6 cloves
1 onion, sliced
1 teaspoon saffron threads, infused
    in 2 tablespoons boiling water,
    for 10 minutes
450 ml/¾ pint salted water

1 Wash the rice thoroughly under cold running water, then leave to soak in cold water for 30 minutes; drain.
2 Melt the butter or ghee in a large pan and fry the spices for a few seconds. Add the onion and fry, stirring, until golden. Add the drained soaked rice and fry for 2–3 minutes.
3 Add the saffron with its infused water and the measured water, stir and bring to the boil. Cover and cook gently for 20 minutes, or until the rice is tender and the liquid has been absorbed. Transfer to a warmed serving dish.

Serves 4
Preparation time: 35 minutes
Cooking time: 30 minutes

Parsee Pilau Rice

This rice dish goes particularly well with rich curries such as Lamb and Vegetable Curry (see page 46) or Chicken Bhuna (see page 70).

1 Heat the ghee in a large, heavy-based frying pan. Stir in the cardamom pods, cloves, cinnamon stick and peppercorns and fry over a gentle heat, stirring constantly, for 2 minutes, until fragrant. Add the saffron threads and rice to the pan and fry, stirring constantly, for 1 further minute.
2 Add the salt, orange flower water, if using, and water. Stir well to mix. Bring to the boil, then reduce the heat, cover the pan and leave the rice to cook gently for 15 minutes without removing the lid.
3 Remove the pan from the heat and lightly loosen the rice grains with a fork. (All the water should have been absorbed.) Stir the sultanas into the rice, cover the pan with a clean, dry tea towel and allow the rice to cook in its own heat for a further 5 minutes.
4 Just before serving, stir the cashews and pistachios into the rice. Serve hot.

Serves 4–6
Preparation time: 10 minutes
Cooking time: 25 minutes

2 tablespoons ghee
6 cardamom pods, bruised
5 cloves
7 cm/3 inch piece cinnamon stick, broken in half
¼ teaspoon black peppercorns, lightly crushed
¼ teaspoon saffron threads
375 g/12 oz basmati rice
¾ teaspoon salt
½ teaspoon orange flower water (optional)
600 ml/1 pint water
25 g/1 oz sultanas
25 g/1 oz roasted cashew nuts
25 g/1 oz pistachio nuts

Biryani

500 g/1 lb basmati rice
8 tablespoons ghee or vegetable oil
10 cm/4 inch piece cinnamon stick
8 cardamom pods
12 cloves
4 garlic cloves, crushed
3.5 cm/1½ inch piece fresh root
   ginger, chopped
1 teaspoon fennel seeds
½ teaspoon chilli powder
1 kg/2 lb boned leg of lamb, cubed
300 g/10 oz natural yogurt
150 ml/¼ pint water
2 teaspoons salt
½ teaspoon saffron threads, infused
   in 3 tablespoons boiling water,
   for 10 minutes
TO GARNISH:
2 tablespoons ghee or oil
1 large onion, sliced
4 tablespoons flaked almonds
4 tablespoons sultanas

1 Wash the basmati rice thoroughly under cold running water, then leave to soak in cold water for 30 minutes.
2 Heat 6 tablespoons of the ghee or oil in a large pan. Add the cinnamon, cardamoms and cloves and fry for a few seconds, stirring. When the spices have released their fragrance, stir in the garlic, ginger, fennel seeds and chilli powder. Fry for 5 minutes, stirring constantly.
3 Add the cubes of lamb and fry well on all sides. Stir in the yogurt a teaspoon at a time, allowing each spoonful to be absorbed before adding the next. Add the water and half the salt, cover and simmer for 40 minutes, or until the lamb is tender.
4 Meanwhile, fill another large pan two-thirds full with water and bring to the boil. Drain the soaking basmati rice and add to the pan with the remaining salt. Boil for 3 minutes, then drain.
5 Put the remaining ghee or oil in a large casserole, cover the base with some of the rice and sprinkle with a little saffron water, then cover with a layer of the yogurty lamb. Repeat the layers, finishing with rice. Pour in any liquid from the lamb, cover closely with a foil-lined lid and cook in a preheated oven, 190°C/375°F/Gas Mark 5, for 25–30 minutes, or until the rice is tender.
6 Meanwhile, prepare the garnish. Heat the ghee or oil in a small frying pan, add the onion and fry until golden. Remove from the pan and set aside. Add the almonds and sultanas to the pan and fry until the almonds are lightly browned and the sultanas plump.
7 Transfer the biryani to a warmed serving dish and sprinkle with the onion, almonds and sultanas to serve.

Serves 4–6
Preparation time: 40 minutes
Cooking time: 1 ¼–1 ½ hours
Oven temperature: 190°C/375°F/Gas Mark 5

'From small beginnings come great things.'

Proverb

Cucumber and Mint Raita

175 g/6 oz natural yogurt
75 g/3 oz cucumber, chopped
2 tablespoons chopped fresh mint
pinch of ground cumin
lemon juice, to taste
salt

This popular classic Indian accompaniment has a cool, refreshing flavour, which complements the heat of spicy dishes.

1 Place the yogurt, cucumber, mint, cumin and lemon juice in a bowl. Add salt to taste and mix gently to combine.
2 Leave the raita to stand for 30 minutes before serving to allow the flavours to develop.

Serves 4
Preparation time: 10 minutes, plus standing

Banana and Coconut Raita

175 g/6 oz natural yogurt
2 small bananas, thinly sliced
2 tablespoons desiccated coconut, toasted
pinch of chilli powder
lemon juice, to taste
salt

1 Place the yogurt, bananas, coconut, chilli powder, lemon juice and a little salt in a bowl and mix gently to combine.
2 Taste and adjust the seasoning, if necessary. Serve the raita immediately as an accompaniment to curries.

Serves 4
Preparation time: 10 minutes

Aubergine Pickle

Some Indian grocers sell split mustard seeds, but if these are unavailable, use ordinary mustard seeds instead.

1 Place the cubed aubergine in a colander, sprinkle over the salt and set aside for 30 minutes, to allow the moisture to be drawn out of the aubergine.

2 Heat the oil in a large, heavy-based frying pan, add the turmeric, cumin, ground coriander, split mustard seeds and chilli powder and fry over a gentle heat, stirring, for 3 minutes, until fragrant.

3 Add the ginger, garlic, chillies and vinegar and stir well. Simmer gently for 10 minutes, stirring occasionally.

4 Add the drained aubergine cubes and the sugar to the pan. Mix well and cook over a moderate heat, stirring occasionally, for 35 minutes, or until the aubergine is very soft and all the flavours are well combined.

5 Ladle the aubergine pickle into sterilized jars, seal and label. This pickle will keep well for 2–3 months.

Makes about 875 g/1¾ lb
Preparation time: 20 minutes, plus standing
Cooking time: 50 minutes

375 g/12 oz aubergines, cut into
    1 cm/½ inch cubes
1 tablespoon salt
75 ml/3 fl oz vegetable oil
1 teaspoon turmeric
1 teaspoon ground cumin
1 teaspoon ground coriander
1 teaspoon split mustard seeds
1 tablespoon chilli powder
5 cm/2 inch piece fresh root
    ginger, grated
4 garlic cloves, crushed
4 red chillies, deseeded and thinly
    sliced
4 green chillies, deseeded and
    thinly sliced
250 ml/8 fl oz white wine vinegar
100 g/3½ oz soft brown sugar

Mango Chutney   *pictured*

250 g/8 oz dried mangoes, covered in cold water and soaked overnight
1 teaspoon chilli powder
6 cardamom pods, bruised
3 cloves
1 teaspoon black mustard seeds
1 teaspoon coriander seeds, lightly crushed
5 black peppercorns, lightly crushed
1 small cinnamon stick, broken in half
375 g/12 oz fresh mango flesh, cut into 1 cm/½ inch cubes
1 large garlic clove, thinly sliced
½ teaspoon salt
300 ml/½ pint white wine vinegar
375 g/12 oz caster sugar
poppadums, to serve (optional)

1 Drain the dried mangoes, reserving 300 ml/½ pint of the soaking liquid, and cut the mangoes into 1.5 cm/¾ inch pieces.
2 Place the chilli powder, cardamom pods, cloves, mustard and coriander seeds, peppercorns and cinnamon stick in a large, heavy-based frying pan. Dry-fry the spices over a gentle heat, stirring frequently, for 2–3 minutes, until fragrant.
3 Add the reserved mango soaking liquid, the dried and the fresh mango pieces, the garlic, salt and vinegar to the spices in the pan. Bring the mixture to the boil, then reduce the heat and simmer gently for 10 minutes, stirring occasionally.
4 Add the sugar and stir over a gentle heat until it has dissolved. Increase the heat and boil the chutney, stirring frequently, until it is thick – this will take about 40 minutes.
5 Ladle the chutney into sterilized jars. Seal, label and store for 2–3 months. Serve with poppadums, if liked, or as an accompaniment to curries.

Makes about 1 kg/2 lb
Preparation time: 20 minutes, plus soaking
Cooking time: 55 minutes

Pineapple Chutney

1 large, ripe pineapple, peeled, cored and chopped into small pieces
3 shallots, chopped
1 green chilli, deseeded and finely chopped
1 tablespoon finely chopped fresh root ginger
25 g/1 oz raisins
125 g/4 oz soft brown sugar
125 ml/4 fl oz distilled malt vinegar
¼ teaspoon salt

1 Place the prepared pineapple with all the other ingredients in a heavy-based pan. Cook over a moderate heat, stirring constantly, until the sugar has dissolved. Bring the mixture to the boil, then reduce the heat a little and boil steadily for 8–10 minutes, stirring occasionally, until most of the liquid has evaporated and the chutney is thick.
2 Pour the hot chutney into sterilized jars. Seal, label and store. Once opened, the chutney will keep well for 3–4 weeks in the refrigerator. Serve with poppadums or as an accompaniment to curries.

Makes about 475 g/15 oz
Preparation time: 10 minutes
Cooking time: 15 minutes

Aubergine Chutney

1 large aubergine
1 small onion, finely chopped
3 green chillies, finely chopped
1 cm/½ inch piece fresh root
 ginger, cut into fine strips
2 tablespoons thick coconut milk
½ teaspoon salt
4 tablespoons lemon juice

This chutney is not overly spicy, largely because of the addition of coconut milk. It makes a good accompaniment to spicy meat or vegetable dishes.

1 Place the whole aubergine on a baking sheet and cook in a preheated oven, 180°C/350°F/Gas Mark 4, for 30 minutes, or until soft. Leave to cool slightly, then slit it open and scoop out the flesh into a bowl.
2 Mash the aubergine with a fork and mix in the remaining ingredients. Taste the chutney and adjust the seasoning. Serve chilled.

Serves 4
Preparation time: 10 minutes, plus chilling
Cooking time: 30 minutes
Oven temperature: 180°C/350°F/Gas Mark 4

Naan

15 g/½ oz fresh yeast
¼ teaspoon sugar
2 tablespoons warm water
500 g/1 lb self-raising flour
1 teaspoon salt
150 ml/¼ pint tepid milk
150 g/5 oz natural yogurt, at room
 temperature
2 tablespoons melted ghee, butter
 or vegetable oil
TO GARNISH:
2–3 tablespoons melted ghee
1 tablespoon poppy or sesame
 seeds

Naan bread is made with leavened flour and is probably the most popular of Indian breads.

1 Put the yeast in a small bowl with the sugar and warm water. Mix well until the yeast has dissolved, then leave in a warm place for 15 minutes, or until the mixture is frothy.
2 Sift the flour and salt into a large bowl. Make a well in the centre and pour in the yeast mixture, the milk, yogurt and melted ghee, butter or oil. Mix well to a smooth dough and turn on to a lightly floured surface. Knead well for about 10 minutes, until smooth and elastic. Place in the bowl, cover with a damp tea towel and leave to rise in a warm place for 1–1½ hours, or until doubled in size.
3 Turn the dough on to a lightly floured surface, knead for a few minutes, then divide it into 6 pieces. Pat each piece into a round.
4 Arrange on warmed baking sheets and cook in a preheated oven, 240°C/475°F/Gas Mark 9, for 10 minutes. Brush with melted ghee or butter and sprinkle with the poppy or sesame seeds. Serve warm.

Makes 6
Preparation time: 30 minutes, plus standing and rising
Cooking time: 10 minutes
Oven temperature: 240°C/475°F/Gas Mark 9

Puri

Like the Chapati (see page 124), the puri is made with ata flour but it is smaller — only 10 cm/4 inches in diameter — and deep-fried, which makes the bread puff up. Serve them alone as a snack or as an accompaniment to curries.

250 g/8 oz ata or plain wholemeal flour
1 tablespoon ghee
250 ml/8 fl oz warm water
vegetable oil, for deep-frying
Aromatic Salt (see page 100)

1 Place the flour, ghee and water in a large bowl and mix to a soft dough. Knead for about 10 minutes, then leave it to stand for about 30 minutes.

2 Divide the dough into 16 pieces. With lightly oiled hands, shape each one into a ball and then roll out on a lightly oiled surface to make 10 cm/4 inch circles.

3 Heat the oil in a deep pan to 190°C/375°F, or until a cube of bread browns in 30 seconds. Deep-fry the puris one at a time in the oil for 20 seconds, or until they puff up like balloons. Remove each one from the oil as soon as it is ready, sprinkle with aromatic salt and serve immediately.

Makes 16
Preparation time: 20 minutes, plus standing
Cooking time: 5–10 minutes

'Bread is the staff of life.'

Proverb

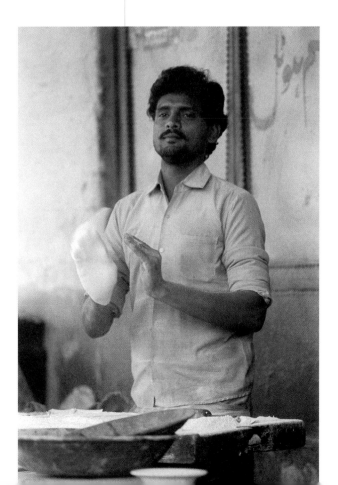

Chapati

500 g/1 lb ata or plain wholemeal
    flour
warm water, to mix
Aromatic Salt (see page 100)
melted butter, for brushing
    (optional)

The staple bread of northern and central India, the chapati is a very thin unleavened round bread, about 15 cm/6 inches in diameter, made from fine-ground hard wholemeal flour (ata flour) and dry-cooked on a griddle or heavy-based frying pan.

1 Mix the flour in a large bowl with enough water to make a soft, pliable dough. Leave to stand for about 30 minutes.
2 Divide the dough into 8 pieces. Roll out each piece on a lightly floured surface to a circle about 18–20 cm/7–8 inches in diameter.
3 Heat a large, heavy-based frying pan over a fairly high heat. Place the chapatis on the dry pan one at a time. After 20–30 seconds, characteristic dark blistering patches appear.
4 Turn the chapati over and cook the other side for about 30 seconds. Sprinkle with aromatic salt and brush with a little melted butter, if liked. Serve promptly or they cool and harden.

Makes 8
Preparation time: 10 minutes, plus standing
Cooking time: 8 minutes

Paratha

The paratha is a wholemeal bread, similar to the Chapati (see page 124), except that it contains ghee, which gives it a flaky texture. Parathas are thicker than chapatis and shallow-fried, as opposed to dry cooked.

1 Mix the flour and salt in a large bowl with enough water to make a soft pliable dough. Knead for 10 minutes, then cover and leave to stand for about 30 minutes.

2 Knead the dough again, then divide into 6 pieces. Roll out each piece on a lightly floured surface into a thin round. Brush with melted ghee or oil and fold in half, brush the top with more ghee or oil and fold in half again. Carefully roll out again to a circle about 3 mm/⅛ inch thick.

3 Lightly grease a griddle or heavy-based frying pan with a little ghee or oil and place over a moderate heat. Add a paratha and cook for 1 minute. Lightly brush the top with a little melted ghee or oil and turn over. Brush all round the edge with ghee or butter and cook until golden. Remove from the pan and keep warm while cooking the rest. Serve warm.

Makes 6
Preparation time: 30 minutes, plus standing
Cooking time: 15 minutes

250 g/8 oz ata or plain wholemeal
   flour
1 teaspoon salt
about 200 ml/7 fl oz water
50–75 g/2–3 oz ghee, melted, or
   1–1½ tablespoons vegetable oil

desserts &
drinks

Climate, local custom and the availability of local products has affected the evolution of Indian sweet cookery. Desserts from western and southern India, for example, feature coconut, while in the wheat-growing areas of the north there are more dishes made with flour and wheat products, such as semolina. Nowadays, everyday meals in India generally end with fresh fruit, which is refreshing and cleansing and makes a perfect conclusion to a spicy meal. Desserts and sweetmeats are usually reserved for festive occasions.

Indian Rice Pudding

75 g/3 oz long-grain rice
1.8 litres/3 pints milk
50 g/2 oz sultanas (optional)
caster sugar, to taste
150 ml/¼ pint single cream
TO DECORATE:
lightly crushed cardamom seeds
rose petals

This Indian variation on rice pudding, flavoured with sultanas and decorated with rose petals, is absolutely wonderful.

1 Place the rice and 1 litre/1¾ pints of the milk in a heavy-based pan. Cook gently at simmering point for 45 minutes to 1 hour, until most of the milk has been absorbed.
2 Add the remaining milk and the sultanas, if using, stir well and continue simmering until thickened. Remove from the heat and add sugar to taste.
3 Leave until completely cold, stirring occasionally to prevent a skin forming, then stir in the cream.
4 Turn into small dishes and serve cold, sprinkled with crushed cardamom seeds and rose petals.

Serves 4
Preparation time: 5 minutes, plus chilling
Cooking time: about 1 hour

'There is no tree but bears some fruit.'

Proverb

Semolina Barfi *pictured*

50 g/2 oz fine semolina
125 g/4 oz granulated sugar
450 ml/¾ pint milk
50 g/2 oz butter
10 cardamom pods, peeled and crushed
75 g/3 oz blanched almonds, halved and toasted

1 Place the semolina and sugar in a heavy-based pan and gradually stir in the milk until smooth. Add the butter in small pieces. Bring to the boil, stirring, then simmer for 3–4 minutes, until thickened, stirring occasionally to prevent sticking. Add the cardamoms and continue cooking for another 10 minutes, until the mixture leaves the side of the pan.
2 Spread the mixture on a buttered plate or in a shallow dish to a thickness of 1–2.5 cm/½–1 inch. Leave until almost cold, then decorate with the almonds.
3 Serve cold, cut into slices or squares.

Serves 4–6
Preparation time: 15 minutes, plus cooling
Cooking time: 20 minutes

Almond Barfi

750 ml/1¼ pints milk
50 g/2 oz caster sugar
50 g/2 oz ground almonds
6 cardamom pods, peeled and crushed

In this imaginative milk pudding recipe, the milk is cooked very slowly until it becomes thick and lumpy, and is then flavoured with sugar, ground almonds and crushed cardamoms.

1 Pour the milk into a large, heavy-based pan and cook for about 1¼ hours over a gentle heat, until it is reduced to a thick, lumpy consistency. Stir occasionally and be careful not to let the milk burn.
2 Stir in the caster sugar, then add the ground almonds and cook for 2 minutes. Pour the mixture into a buttered shallow dish and sprinkle with the crushed cardamoms. Serve warm, cut into squares or diamond shapes.

Serves 4
Preparation time: 10 minutes
Cooking time: 1¼ hours

Yogurt Dessert

1 kg/2 lb natural yogurt
¼ teaspoon saffron threads
about 2 tablespoons caster sugar
about 1 tablespoon rosewater
TO DECORATE:
1–2 teaspoons cardamom seeds,
    crushed
1 tablespoon pistachio nuts, shelled
    and chopped

This yogurt-based dessert is flavoured with saffron and rosewater.

1 Turn the yogurt into a sieve lined with muslin and leave to drip over a bowl for 6 hours. Put the dried curds — there will be about 300 g/10 oz – into a bowl and beat in the saffron. Add the sugar to taste – add a little more if you like, but it should not be too sweet.
2 Mix in the rosewater, a little at a time, until the mixture resembles thick cream. Cover and chill until required.
3 Spoon into individual bowls and decorate with the crushed cardamom seeds and chopped pistachios to serve.

Serves 4
Preparation time: 10 minutes, plus standing and chilling

Milk Dessert

1.8 litres/3 pints full cream milk
3–4 tablespoons caster sugar
TO DECORATE:
2 leaves varq (silver leaf)
edible flower petals

1 Cook the milk in a large, heavy-based pan for about 1¼ hours, until it is reduced to a thick, lumpy consistency. Stir occasionally and be careful not to let the milk burn.
2 Add the sugar and continue cooking for 10 minutes.
3 Spread the mixture on a lightly buttered plate – it should be a lightly cream coloured, softly-set toffee.
4 Cut into wedges and serve cold, decorated with strips of varq and edible flower petals.

Serves 4–6
Preparation time: 5 minutes
Cooking time: 1 hour 25 minutes

Cook's Note
Varq is edible silver leaf, often used in Indian cooking for decorative purposes. Available from specialist Indian food stores, it is very fragile and should be handled with care.

Almond Ice Cream

Milk, sugar and cream are combined with ground almonds to produce a frozen dessert.

250 g/8 oz blanched almonds
1.8 litres/3 pints milk
250 g/8 oz caster sugar
300 ml/½ pint double cream
2 tablespoons rosewater

1 Place the almonds in a bowl, cover with cold water and set aside. Reserve 300 ml/½ pint of the milk and bring the rest to the boil in a large, heavy-based or non-stick pan. Simmer until the milk is reduced by half, stirring from time to time to ensure that any skin or solids that cling to the side of the pan are well mixed in.
2 Drain the almonds and place three-quarters of them in a blender or food processor with the reserved milk. Blend the mixture for a few seconds until the almonds are roughly ground; the mixture should be crunchy. Add the almond mixture and caster sugar to the pan of milk and continue simmering for a further 10–20 minutes, stirring constantly. Remove the pan from the heat and leave to cool to room temperature, then place in the refrigerator until well chilled.
3 Roughly chop the remaining almonds and add them to the chilled milk mixture with the double cream and rosewater, stirring thoroughly so that the ingredients are well mixed. Pour into moulds and freeze until solid.
4 Transfer to the refrigerator 20 minutes before serving, then turn out and serve.

Serves 8
Preparation time: 1 hour, plus chilling and freezing
Cooking time: about 40 minutes

Mango Ice Cream *pictured*

400 g/13 oz can condensed milk
300 ml/½ pint double cream
125 g/4 oz granulated sugar
1 tablespoon roughly chopped
  almonds
1 tablespoon roughly chopped
  pistachio nuts, plus extra
  to decorate
400 g/13 oz can mango slices or
  pulp, some reserved and
  chopped to decorate
1 tablespoon kewra water or
  lemon juice

1 Boil the milk and cream together in a large heavy-based pan with the sugar, stirring constantly until the sugar dissolves, then leave to simmer over a very low heat for about 30 minutes.
2 Stir in the almonds and pistachios, and cool to room temperature by standing the pan in a bowl of cold water.
3 If using mango slices, drain off half the juice from the can and crush the slices with the remaining juice. Reserve some to decorate.
4 Add the mango to the milk mixture, then add the kewra water or lemon juice and beat well. Pour into moulds and freeze until the solid. Turn out, decorate with pistachios and mango and serve.

Serves 4
Preparation time: 20 minutes, plus freezing
Cooking time: 40 minutes

Cook's Note
Kewra water is an essence distilled from a palm-like plant called pandanus, and is available from good Indian grocers.

Pistachio Ice Cream

125 g/4 oz unsalted pistachio nuts,
  shelled, plus extra to decorate
400 g/13 oz can condensed milk
300 ml/½ pint double cream
125 g/4 oz caster sugar
2 eggs, separated
2 drops almond essence
2 drops green food colouring
  (optional)

1 Place the pistachios in a bowl, cover with cold water and set aside.
2 Heat the condensed milk in a pan and add the double cream and the caster sugar, stirring until the sugar dissolves. Beat the egg yolks into the mixture, together with the almond essence and the green colouring, if using, then leave the mixture to simmer gently.
3 Drain the pistachios and rub off the skins. Chop the nuts finely and add to the pan, beating in well. Bring to the boil, then leave to cool to room temperature. Place in the refrigerator until the mixture is nearly set.
4 Whisk the egg whites in a clean bowl until they form peaks. Fold the beaten egg whites into the chilled mixture until evenly mixed, then pour into moulds and freeze until firm. Turn out and serve decorated with chopped pistachio nuts.

Serves 4
Preparation time: 40 minutes, plus freezing
Cooking time: 15 minutes

Batter Coils in Syrup

375 g/12 oz plain flour
150 g/5 oz natural yogurt
25 g/1 oz dried yeast
500 g/1 lb granulated sugar
600 ml/1 pint water
pinch of saffron
6 cardamom pods
6 cloves
vegetable oil, for deep-frying
icing sugar, to dust

1 Sift the flour into a bowl and add the yogurt, yeast and enough cold water to form a batter the consistency of double cream. Cover and leave in a warm place for about 4 hours to ferment.

2 Dissolve the sugar in the water in a pan over a low heat with the saffron, cardamoms and cloves. Bring to the boil and cook to reduce the liquid and produce a heavy syrup. Set aside.

3 Heat the vegetable oil in a large pan to 190°C/375°F, or until a cube of bread browns in 30 seconds. Pour the batter in a steady stream through an icing bag, to form coil shapes in the hot oil below. Make a few coils at a time and cook for about 1 minute, turning, until they are light brown and crisp.

4 Remove the coils from the pan with a slotted spoon, drain on kitchen paper, then immerse in the syrup for about 5 minutes.

5 Remove them from the syrup; drain and dust with icing sugar. Serve immediately while warm and crisp.

Serves 4
Preparation time: 20 minutes, plus fermenting
Cooking time: 20 minutes

Sweet Lassi

A yogurt and milk drink that is blended with rosewater and ice cubes.

1 Place the yogurt, milk and kewra water or rosewater in a blender or food processor with sugar to taste. Add some ice cubes and blend until the ice cubes have almost disappeared.
2 Pour into tall glasses and serve immediately.

Serves 4
Preparation time: 5 minutes

300 ml/½ pint natural yogurt
300 ml/½ pint milk
½ teaspoon kewra water or
  rosewater
sugar
ice cubes

Salted Lassi

1 Place the cumin seeds in a heavy-based pan set over a fairly high heat and dry-roast for 1–2 minutes. Cool slightly, then grind using an electric spice mill or a pestle and mortar.
2 Place the yogurt, milk, lemon juice, dry-roasted and ground cumin and salt into a blender or food processor. Add some ice cubes and blend briefly. Taste and add more salt if necessary, then pour into tall glasses and serve immediately.

Serves 4
Preparation time: 5 minutes
Cooking time: 1–2 minutes

I teaspoon cumin seeds
300 ml/½ pint natural yogurt
300 ml/½ pint chilled milk
4 tablespoons lemon juice
½–I teaspoon salt
ice cubes

Rice and Milk Dessert *pictured*

25 g/1 oz basmati rice
150 ml/¼ pint water
600 ml/1 pint milk
125 g/4 oz sugar
5 drops kewra water
25 g/1 oz mixed pistachio nuts and
   almonds, chopped, plus extra
   to decorate

1 Soak the rice in a bowl containing the water for 1½ hours. Cook the rice in a large pan of boiling water for 15 minutes, then drain.
2 Heat the milk slowly in a pan and stir in the rice. Place the mixture in a blender or food processor and blend to a smooth paste. Return to the pan, heat gently and stir until the mixture begins to thicken. Remove from the heat and add the sugar.
3 When the sugar is fully dissolved, bring to the boil and simmer for 2 minutes. Leave to cool, then add the kewra water and the chopped pistachios and almonds.
4 Serve chilled, decorated with almonds and pistachios.

Serves 4
Preparation time: 10 minutes, plus soaking and chilling
Cooking time: 10–15 minutes

Carrot Halva

1.2 litres/2 pints milk
250 g/8 oz carrots, finely grated
75 g/3 oz butter
1 tablespoon golden syrup
125 g/4 oz granulated sugar
50 g/2 oz sultanas or raisins
TO DECORATE:
1 teaspoon cardamom seeds,
   crushed
2 leaves varq (silver leaf)

1 Place the milk and grated carrot in a heavy-based pan and cook over a high heat, stirring occasionally, until the liquid has evaporated. Add the butter, syrup, sugar and dried fruit. Stir until the butter and sugar have melted, then cook for 15–20 minutes, stirring frequently, until the mixture starts to leave the side of the pan.
2 Pour into a shallow buttered dish and spread evenly. Decorate with crushed cardamom seeds and strips of varq. Cut into slices and serve warm or cold.

Serves 4–6
Preparation time: 10 minutes
Cooking time: 45–50 minutes

glossary

ANISEED
These are the seeds of the anise plant, which is an aromatic plant that originated in India and Egypt. Aniseed has a liquorice flavour and is often used in curries and marinades.

BASMATI
This rice is a special variety of Indian rice that has small, long grains and a distinctive flavour. It works particularly well in pilau dishes and in desserts. It should always be soaked in cold water for about 30 minutes before use.

CARDAMOM
This plant is from south-western India and the capsules contain seeds that are dried and then used as a spice. It is quite a common ingredient in Indian cookery and it is most often used as a flavouring for rice and cakes.

CHICKPEA
This is a plant with rounded edible seeds enclosed in pods. If dried, chickpeas should always be soaked before use, but they are also available precooked and canned. Chickpeas are rich in carbohydrates, proteins, calcium and iron.

CHILLI POWDER
This varies according to its country of origin. Indian chilli powder is made from the dried and ground flesh and seeds of red chillies. It is similar to cayenne pepper.

CINNAMON
This is obtained by drying and rolling up the bark of cinnamon trees. This makes a tube that has a sweet aroma and a hot spicy flavour. It is also available in powder form.

CLOVES
These are the dried flower buds of the clove tree. Cloves are used in many meat dishes, as well as in marinades, pickles and as an ingredient in spice mixtures.

COCONUT MILK
This is widely used in Indian cookery. It can be made either using desiccated or fresh coconut, but it is readily available from supermarkets in cans.

CORIANDER
Coriander has an intense flavour and aroma. The bright green leaves make an attractive garnish for dishes and the leaves, roots and seeds are all used in cooking.

CUMIN
The seeds of an aromatic plant, with a hot and slightly bitter taste. Cumin blends well with coriander and other spices. It is an ideal flavouring for fish and prawns.

CURRY LEAVES
These are green leaves that are from a tree that is found in India and Sri Lanka. They are used both fresh and dry, but are only included in dishes as a flavouring and are removed before serving.

FENNEL SEEDS
These are light greenish-brown in colour and are used widely in Indian cookery, particularly with meat, fish and vegetables. Whole roasted fennel seeds are also chewed in India after a meal to freshen the palate.

FENUGREEK POWDER
The fenugreek plant is a member of the pea family. It produces long, slender pods that contain flattened brown seeds. These are roasted and ground and used as a flavouring in curries. It is also one of the main ingredients in curry powder.

GARAM MASALA
This is mild, sweet seasoning from northern India that is available in many supermarkets and Indian food stores. It usually contains cardamom, cinnamon, cloves, cumin, coriander and black peppercorns.

GHEE
This is clarified butter that can be heated to higher temperatures than other oils, without burning. It can also be stored for a lot longer than butter. There are two types of ghee: pure (a dairy product) and vegetable ghee.

GINGER
This plant originated in south-east Asia. It has underground stems that can be used fresh or powdered. In India, it is used to flavour meat, fish, rice and vegetables, to season curries and to flavour tea.

GRAM FLOUR
This is made from lentils and is used in Indian cookery to thicken sauces and also to make pakoras. It is a light golden colour and has a distinctive taste.

LENTILS
These are small, round dry seeds that are always eaten shelled and cooked. They originated in central Asia and are a staple food in many countries.

MASOOR DHAL
This a small, round dried lentil. They should be cooked before being added to dishes, or they can be cooked with onion and spices as a dish on their own. Red lentils are used in many Indian dishes.

MINT
A fragrant herb with a strong fresh flavour. There are 25 different varieties of mint, all with bright green leaves and small white flowers. It is used in many Indian dishes, especially with lamb.

MOONG DHAL
This is a dried whole or split yellow bean, which has a green skin and yellow flesh. The beans are used in soups and are more popular in northern India than in the south.

MUNG BEANS
These come from a bean plant called haricot mungo, which originated in the Far East. It has small green yellow or brown seeds.

OKRA
This is a tropical plant that is rich in vitamin C, calcium, phosphorus and iron. It is available all year round and can also be bought dried and in cans. It can be cooked whole or sliced and is popular in Indian cookery.

ORANGE FLOWER WATER
This is a delicate flavouring that enhances the flavour of many dishes, including rice for a dessert.

PANIR
This is an Indian curd cheese used in cooking. It is available from Indian specialist food stores. Panir goes particularly well with vegetable dishes made with spinach or peas.

PAPRIKA
This is a spicy seasoning that is ground from a sweet pepper variety. Only small amounts of paprika should be bought at a time and it should be replaced often, as its flavour and colour deteriorate quickly.

ROSEWATER
This is used to flavour ice cream and pastries, as well as wines. It is available from the baking section of supermarkets and delicatessens.

SAFFRON
This spice consists of the dried stigmas of the saffron crocus. It has a pungent smell and a bitter flavour. It is the most expensive and highly prized of all spices and is available ground or as whole threads. Many recipes require saffron threads to be infused in boiling water before use.

TURMERIC
Turmeric belongs to the same family as ginger and grows wild in countries in southern Asia. It has an attractive yellow colour, that is similar to saffron and it is used both as a spice and a colorant. It has a more bitter taste than saffron.

TAMARIND
The fruit of an evergreen tree that originated in west Africa. The pods are brown, long and wide and contain a pulp with a few hard seeds in it. In Indian cuisine, the pulp of dried tamarind is a major ingredient in many spice mixtures and is also used in chutneys.

VARQ
This is edible silver leaf, used for decorative purposes. It is fragile and should be handled with great care. Varq is available from specialist Indian food stores.

index